Love Comes When Least Expected

MISSIONARY LOVE STORIES

Olga Warner Penzin

WESTBOW
PRESS®
A DIVISION OF THOMAS NELSON
& ZONDERVAN

WestBow Press books may be ordered through booksellers or by contacting:

WestBow Press
A Division of Thomas Nelson & Zondervan
1663 Liberty Drive
Bloomington, IN 47403
www.westbowpress.com
1 (866) 928-1240

ISBN: 978-1-5127-3624-3 (sc)
ISBN: 978-1-5127-3626-7 (hc)
ISBN: 978-1-5127-3625-0 (e)

Library of Congress Control Number: 2016905254

Print information available on the last page.

WestBow Press rev. date: 04/19/2016

Contents

What's Here and Why (Introduction) vii
    Olga Warner Penzin

Significant Words

"But Lord, If I Go to the Mission Field, I'll Never Get
    Married."...1
    Elaine Townsend

"You Will Marry Egbert!" 13
    Hattie Dyk

"Dear Lord, Please Give Jan A Husband. She Needs One.".....28
    Jan Townsend

"We Have Your Tickets, But--"....................................50
    Martha and Bob Tripp

"I Have Planned It, Surely I Will Do It." 75
    Beverly Wolfenden

"This Is My Daughter. She's Twenty One." 87
    Mary Jane and Ron Michaels

"You Have A Ticket. I Suggest You Use It."............................ 101
    Wanda and John Davies

What's Here and Why
Introduction

W) here does a person meet that 'special someone' who will become his or her life partner? For some the answer is found at churches, Bible colleges, and other places where Christians gather. These places offer the possibility of meeting like-minded young people.

But if he or she doesn't meet the 'right' person in that kind of place, what then? In verses 3-7 of Psalm 37 (KJV) we find God's promises of what He will do when we obey His admonitions to "trust...delight...commit...rest...and wait."

Young people who answer God's call to the foreign mission field may feel that their possibilities of finding a life partner are severely limited. But behind every married couple on the mission field is a love story. Many started during childhood, high school or college. The stories included here don't start that way, but each one has some kind of unique twist. God must have smiled with satisfaction as they developed. Many include humorous incidents. Together they provide a reminder that God has all kinds of ways of meeting our needs, and His ways are best.

Other kinds of love, besides romantic love, shine through these stories, including love for God and love for the work to which He has called each individual. These stories are of members of Wycliffe Bible Translators. I first heard of Elaine Townsend's and Hattie Dyk's experiences as told by them at large public gatherings, and I thought, "These stories are too good not to be published." Later Elaine and Hattie related them to me personally, as did the others recorded here. Each one told their stories freely and gladly with the understanding that I hoped to publish their words. This is by no means an exhaustive collection of missionary love stories. Certainly, other members of Wycliffe and members of other mission organizations could add their fascinating adventures.

A little of the history of Wycliffe Bible Translators as it relates to their experiences is included, as well as insights into living environments and kinds of work they were doing.

It was my plan to finish the project of publishing this book while all of the principals were still living but I was unable to do so.

I hope these stories will provide entertainment and inspiration for people of all ages, especially reminding young people that God delights in providing solutions to all our problems.

It is only with the dedicated work of a friend and volunteer, who shared my vision for the publication, that these stories will finally be published. She also recruited other volunteers, whose expertise has assisted greatly in the completion of this manuscript. All helped by providing research for updated endings and editorial and grammatical edits. My most sincere appreciation goes to all who contributed to this effort.

Olga Warner Penzin

"But Lord, If I Go to the Mission Field, I'll Never Get Married."

*I*n 1942, a tall, dark-haired, blue-eyed young woman named Elaine Mielke taught at a public school in Chicago in a largely Polish neighborhood. While most of America's young men were involved in winning World War II, young ladies were getting along without them and taking their places in offices, banks, factories--all kinds of jobs.

The nation was managing without some of the finer necessities that everyone had gotten used to. Women formed lines at department stores to buy baggy lisle stockings, as silk ones were no longer available. Sugar, among other things, was rationed because of limited supply. Each family was issued books of coupons to be used for purchasing rationed items.

Elaine had been appointed to manage distribution of the ration books and special coupons for sugar for her school's neighborhood. As she told it, "These dear grandmas were coming to get their coupons, and I couldn't speak their language." So she asked a friend, Ann Williams, who spoke Polish to come and help. At coffee break one morning, Ann shared, "Last night I was at Chicago Gospel Tabernacle, where I heard the most wonderful speaker talking about a brand new organization called Wycliffe Bible Translators. His name is Cameron Townsend. They have an institute in Norman, Oklahoma, to teach young people how to reduce languages to writing, and I want to go there this summer. What are you going to do with your summer?"

"My plans are to go to Mexico to improve my Spanish," said Elaine, because she had also been working after school hours at a Mexican mission. But when she heard it cost only $5.00 a week for room and board, she could not resist.

"So I found myself at Norman, a school with only one hundred and thirty students." This was the first year that the Summer Institute of Linguistics (SIL) was held on the campus of the University of Oklahoma. William Cameron Townsend had started the program in 1934 as Camp Wycliffe in a barn near Sulphur Springs, Arkansas, with two students. He was eager to teach others how to learn unwritten languages so that portions of the Bible could be translated as he had done in Guatemala.

In the beginning for lack of better furniture, the students sat on nail kegs. Cameron, as he was more commonly called, had brought his language helper from Guatemala, so that the students could get firsthand experience in hearing and imitating sounds of a language they had never known and could practice analyzing its structure. By 1941, enrollment had reached almost fifty students.

Cameron had gone to Guatemala as a young man in 1917 to sell Spanish Bibles and had walked trails all over Central America, finally settling down in a Guatemalan village among people who spoke Cakchiquel, one of the Mayan languages. He had become concerned because they could not understand the Spanish Scriptures he had distributed, so he was determined to give them God's Word in their own language. Without linguistic training, he persisted until he completed the translation of the New Testament. It was presented to the Cakchiquel Indians in 1931.

During that time, he had married Elvira Malmstrom, a young woman who had also gone to Guatemala to work as a missionary.

In 1942 the small group of enthusiastic budding linguists, who had begun learning some of the unwritten languages of Mexico, got together to incorporate their group. They determined that the name of their organization should be Wycliffe Bible Translators, after John Wycliffe, the first person to translate the Bible into the English language.

Some of these first recruits taught the courses in linguistics at Norman when Elaine attended that summer of 1942. She remembers that they held chapel while sitting on the floor in a sorority house. For the most part, it was a prayer meeting. "The linguists were praying for someone to come and teach the missionary children in Mexico," Elaine relates. "They had no assistance at that time-- no support people and no schoolteacher."

Elaine had majored in education and was also trained to teach mentally handicapped children. About fifteen children, mostly Polish, were in her class in Chicago when she first heard about the linguistics course.

She returned to Chicago after that first-year summer course at Norman, and she was promoted to supervisor of the mentally handicapped children's program for three hundred area schools. However, Elaine felt that the Lord kept speaking to her heart about the need for a teacher for missionary children. Finally she decided to heed that 'call.'

"Many things came into the way though," she recalled. "It took me a whole year to be smart enough to say, 'I will.' My first reaction was to say, 'Well, I support four missionaries, I've got a really good job, and I'm supervisor over all these school programs. You'd rather have my money than me, wouldn't You, Lord?'

"I told Him that so often He must have gotten awfully tired of hearing it. Or maybe He knew I would eventually keep my promise, and He wouldn't let me get by with the excuses.

"Then I said, 'Well Lord, You know if I go to the mission field I'll never have friends like I have here in Chicago, and I can't live without friends. So surely You don't want me to go.' My second objection was that I don't want to look like the missionaries who get their clothes from missionary barrels. But the primary objection was, 'Oh Lord, if I go to the mission field, I'll never get married, and You know I want to get married!'" (According to her daughter Grace, Elaine's firm conviction at that time was that she would never go to the mission field as a single woman and never marry anyone a lot older than she or anyone who had been married before.)

Another hurdle was that her father did not approve. He had a tract box ministry and wanted Elaine to help with that.

The next year, 1943, Elaine attended the second-year summer course at SIL in Norman, Oklahoma, joined Wycliffe as a member, and left for Mexico to teach missionary children. Elaine said that while the Mexicans at the Chicago mission sang to her at the train station as she left, her father cried. Sometime later, however, she heard that he spoke of her work at a Gideon's banquet, saying that he was glad she had not listened to him but obeyed the Lord and followed Him.

Elaine's first assignment in Mexico was to teach three seventh- and eighth-grade children of two Wycliffe families in the Aztec village of Tetelcingo, south of Mexico City. "I was living with the Todd family, the home of two of the girls I taught. We had classes in the home. I enjoyed teaching those three children, but weekends were very, very difficult. I kept thinking that back in Chicago I'd be doing the Mexican mission work, having so many wonderful opportunities to witness, and here I am stuck with these three children. Many times I wanted to quit, but I'm so thankful I didn't give up."

An unpleasant experience during that time became the first personal impact Cameron Townsend had on her life. Elaine said, "I was going to Mexico City three times a week to study Spanish. I would teach in the morning and then catch the bus to the city in the afternoon for the hour-and-a-half trip. The bus stopped right in front of my house."

"One day as I sat on the bus, a guy sat down next to me and asked what I was doing. He offered his help when I told him I studied Spanish in the city. Then he asked when I was going back, and unfortunately I told him.

"Two days later, he came to our home with a bottle of whiskey and wanted me to go out with him. When I refused and told him that I had a friend back in Chicago, he replied, 'Oh well, I've got a wife in Huautla, but that doesn't mean anything.' When he realized I turned him down, he took that bottle of whiskey and threw it against a brick wall. The kids screamed, and I did too. I was afraid because he was a Mexican official.

"When Cameron heard that, he went to the local Mexican government and 'got him off my back.' It was a scary time, and I truly appreciated Cameron's personal attention to my need for help."

This happened in Tetelcingo where Cameron and Elvira Townsend also lived. They attended the same church, and Elaine knew Elvira well. Elaine was impressed with Cameron's love for children, though he and Elvira had none. "At the time I had a home of cement block right behind the Townsend house," said Elaine. "When Cameron would go to South America, I would take care of Elvira. He wanted me to be company for her, and she needed that company because she was sickly--very sickly. That's why she and I were so close."

After teaching the mission children for a year or more, Elaine conducted six-week-long reading campaigns in seventeen different language groups, using primers and other materials prepared by the linguists. Her partner was a lovely young Mexican girl, Esther, who had worked in the kitchen. They traveled by train, by bus and on mule back to the villages.

Elaine mentioned going to the area where Marge Davis and her partner worked on the Cuicatec language and how she experienced the joy of teaching villagers to read God's Word. "It felt like ice cream on the cake or something--the best part of the celebration, because the linguists had done the hard work, and I came along and taught them to read."

In December of 1944, Elvira Townsend died. During the months that followed, there was speculation among the members in Mexico as to whom of the several young ladies who were part of the mission Cameron might choose to take as his next wife.

The group of linguists was headquartered in Mexico City in a former hotel named Quetzalcoatl, later nicknamed the Kettle by visitors who had difficulty pronouncing the Aztec name. At the Center, translation staff members who had business in the city could stay there to have meetings and fellowship.

There were times when Cameron and Elaine were in the city at the same time and began to spend time together. "I had my eye on him for sure," said Elaine. "He had no money to take me on a date, and there was no privacy. We would just take walks together."

Elaine had been calling Cameron 'Uncle Cam' as did other members of Wycliffe, until one day he said, "Elaine, do you suppose you could leave off the word uncle?" "I tried it," she recalled, "and I liked it! That was the first time we connected as just two people."

Another time Cameron called her from Chicago and said, "I love you" in Aztec. She didn't know the language but guessed what it meant and responded "That's nice!" Others had not yet noticed this developing interest between them.

Then one night, translators Neil and Jane Nellis, who lived down the road in Tetelcingo, invited Cameron and Elaine over for a meal. Neil had planned to play chess with Cameron, and Jane was to help Elaine make her bedroom curtains. But when the time came, Cameron said, "No, I think I'll help Elaine make her curtains." So as he sat beside her, Neil and Jane began to see the light. Neil still thought that Mrs. Hull, who was 10 years older than Cam, would be ideal for him.

Elaine recalled thinking, "I am twenty years younger than he, and many others are wondering who he will marry because there were a lot of girls my age in Mexico and elsewhere in the organization."

Elaine also recalled an interesting development. "At another time Adam Johnson, a multimillionaire, came down to Tetelcingo. He decided to drive the car on an outing. Cameron sat in the middle, I was on the end, and Cameron had his cowboy hat over his hand and mine. I didn't know that Adam Johnson noticed that Cam was squeezing my hand the whole time!"

Cameron traveled extensively to Peru at that time to make arrangements with officials for the beginning of linguistic studies in that country. He also traveled to the USA to inspire support for Bible translation and the work involved, as well as sometimes to Canada where another linguistic school was being set up.

At these times he kept in contact with Elaine by mail. His letters included discussions about when they might see each other next, her plans for literacy campaigns in certain areas, her anticipated tonsillectomy, references to Bible passages, and news of other members of the Mexico Branch when he was in Mexico City. But especially, he made sure that Elaine was aware of his feelings for her. Perhaps his many years in Latin America influenced his writing, for his letters contained flowery and poetic language. He even teased her a little.

"Oh, yes," said Elaine. "On top of it, Cameron mentioned in one of those letters that I wasn't supposed to think of John. That was John the official who scared me with his attentions earlier."

In later years Elaine often shared the sentiments of those letters with friends, as when Cameron wrote, "Think of it--a girl marrying a man twenty years older. She's too young, though, to know any better. And if you were to get engaged to some fine young man, I would know then that the Lord wanted me to remain single the rest of my life, and I would be happy in it. But selfishly I would like so very, very much to have you as my very own partner."

7

James and Marty Hefley relate in their book <u>Uncle Cam,</u> how Cameron had nervously asked permission to marry her from Elaine's father, confessing that he had nothing material to offer her. Receiving her father's blessing, Cam had told a friend, Dawson Trotman, of his plan to marry but mentioned his intention to wait three years in order to get the work going in Peru. Trotman approved the marriage but not the wait. Then Cameron asked approval of two special friends in Mexico, Hazael Marroquin, representative of the American Bible Society in Mexico, and revolutionary General Lazaro Cardenas, President of Mexico. Both encouraged him.

During the years when the little group of linguists was getting started in their work in Mexico, General Cardenas governed from 1934 to 1940. He had heard about a *gringo* who was raising lettuce in the town square in Tetelcingo and teaching Indians ways to improve their lives, so he traveled there to assess the situation. This was the beginning of a lasting friendship between President Cardenas and Cameron Townsend which became a vital part of the Townsend/Mielke relationship.

Early in 1945 the first session of Jungle Camp was established in Chiapas, Mexico, close to the Guatemalan border. Cameron was the Director and Elaine was one of the participants. For three months the young volunteers trained for living in primitive situations and acclimating to local culture.

In October of 1945, while Elaine was conducting a literacy campaign in southern Mexico, Cameron wrote, "Will you marry me in March?" She replied promptly and later she shared her reply in part with friends. "For years I have wondered whether the Lord would ever bring across my life a companion I could love with all my heart; one whose interests were the same as mine; one who is thoughtful, understanding, loving, patient, loves children, generous, hospitable, self-sacrificing, a dynamic personality, a leader, a pioneer in the Lord's work; one who practices what he preaches; a man of prayer. All of these qualities I have found in you, so in answer to your question I can gladly say, 'YES.' As far as being willing to undergo hardships, let me assure you that I came to the mission field expecting to endure hardships as a soldier of Jesus Christ; and I shall still be happy to do so."

At a mission conference years later, she related the romantic side of Cameron Townsend. "For Valentine's Day before we were married, while flying on a commercial airliner, Cameron turned a little napkin into a Valentine for me with this verse:

For you I pine, my Valentine. For you I sigh, my cherry pie.

For you I dream, whose eyes so beam, for you I wait, my helpmate great.

And now I write my angel bride, to say I love you, Precious Dove."

In the meantime, Cameron told Elaine he thought she should continue the literacy work and asked that she trust him to make all the arrangements for the wedding. General Cardenas had already agreed to be best man and his wife, Amalia, matron of honor. They wanted the ceremony held in their home on Lake Patzcuaro, in the state of Michoacan, about ten hours' drive from Mexico City.

Cameron's apprehension centered on the invitation list of one-hundred people, which included many Mexican high government officials. Travel arrangements also included those for guests from Chicago and California.

The big day, April 4, 1946, dawned bright and sunny. Family and friends from Chicago and California arrived. Mexico's leading anthropologist, Dr. Manuel Gamio, six generals and other prominent Mexicans were also in attendance. The orchestra played. Amanda Marroquin sang "The Love of God" in Spanish. The local mayor presided. Elaine remembers that the cake was larger than the cake for the British princess who married about the same time--so large they had to remove part of the doorway in order to bring it in. She remembered that seven or eight limousines waited outside.

The short ceremony was soon over and the thirty-year-old Elaine became Senora William Cameron Townsend. The reception seemed a blur of picture posing and hand shaking.

As the bridal couple started for the door, Cam blurted out, "I know what I forgot!" Everyone wanted to know what it was, but Elaine's comment was, "It doesn't matter dear. Whatever it was, I didn't even notice." "But, but" Cam stammered, "I forgot to get a place for us to spend the wedding night!" After some good-natured teasing, Cam's Uncle Al came to the rescue by offering his room at the nearby Don Vasco Hotel.

"We were married in Mexico, and on our honeymoon we took eighteen new recruits to Peru," Elaine remembered. "That's when I knew I married Wycliffe Bible Translators, not just Cameron Townsend. From then on we were a team. We shared all our wedding gifts. All of our wedding money went to pay the rent for the group the first week. It was quite an unusual way to start our marriage. We had nothing to start on. Everybody slept on the floor."

Peru was the second country to which young members of Wycliffe went to study unwritten languages, and Elaine joined Cameron in getting the work started there. They stayed at a hotel in Lima at first, and then they moved to a house where they and all the new recruits lived together. She recalled that her first 'private' home after she was married was out in the jungle as an army tent with a pole through the center.

Later, houses for the Townsends and for others were built near Yarinacocha, a beautiful jungle lake. This became the Jungle Base, a place for translators to live when they came back from their tribal locations.

For many years, as early as 1928, Cameron had been aware that airplanes would be a great help in missionary work. During their time in Peru, as he saw how some translators had spent days of travel on dangerous jungle rivers to reach their tribal locations, he became convinced that planes were absolutely essential to transport the translators in and out of the remote jungle areas. The translators also needed radio contact with the Jungle Base. Reliable and safe air transport and two-way radios would provide a lifeline for them in times of emergency.

The Townsend's first baby, Grace, was born in Lima, Peru. When she was six-weeks' old, Cameron and Elaine traveled with her to Mexico, stopping first for a visit at Jungle Camp. As they took off from Jungle Camp in a small commercial plane, it crashed. Fearing that the plane might catch fire, jungle campers and staff removed them from the plane quickly. As they were lying on the grass nearby, Uncle Cam called for someone to take pictures to document the need for reliable plane service for missionaries. This near-fatal, firsthand experience became the catalyst for the energetic pursuit of Cameron's early vision to illustrate to the Christian public the need for airplanes in mission work.

Baby Grace, snug in a basket, was safe, but Elaine suffered a broken ankle and a back injury, injuries which continued to plague her through the years. Cameron suffered a big gouge in his upper leg. This was one important event that led to the forming of Wycliffe's Jungle Aviation and Radio Service (JAARS) in Peru.

As the work of learning unwritten languages and translating the Bible in the local language spread to other countries throughout the world, the services of JAARS were a part of that mission. An international headquarters for JAARS was established near Waxhaw, North Carolina, where services grew to include many other support needs such as computers, information technology, trucking, construction and maintenance, and non-print media.

There was no limit to the vision and faith Cameron had for breaking new ground, and Elaine was right there with him in every move. Together they made eleven trips to the Soviet Union during his last years. The work is continuing to go forward there.

There is no doubt that he chose the right partner. Elaine was always willing to speak to any group that invited her. When she met someone new, it was her custom to introduce that person to someone else as 'my friend.' One of her excuses for not going to the mission field had been that she wouldn't have friends, but she found friends all over the world.

Together Cameron and Elaine designed their home at the JAARS Center where they are now both interred between the Mexico and the Alphabet museums. The four Townsend children all serve the Lord in one way or another in some mission work.

Occasionally, she quoted her most heart-felt reason for her resistance to the 'call,' "Lord, if I go to the mission field, I'll never get married, and You know I want to get married." Elaine added, "And then I married the boss and was his partner for some thirty-six years!"

"You Will Marry Egbert!"

In times of sadness and great personal loss, most people find it difficult to speak publicly about that which is closest to their hearts and their emotions. Hattie Dyk is one person who defies that classification.

At the memorial service for her husband, Egbert Dyk, following his death in the summer of 2001, numerous friends shared their memories of him and told of the countless ways that he had contributed to their lives.

Then, without hesitation, Hattie stepped to the platform, her white hair curled attractively close to her head complementing the white of her suit jacket. She spoke in her usual high, crisp manner, her words tinted with something, not an accent, just a hint of her first language or of other languages she had studied. She spoke of Egbert's life and what it meant to her. But the most memorable event she shared produced an immediate roar of laughter from the entire assembly. It was the story of the voice she seemed to hear when she was young saying that she would marry Egbert!

On another more private occasion, Hattie, whose maiden name was VanderVos, told her story this way in her charming, idiomatic English, her second language.

"I was born in the Netherlands; and when I was about eleven, my parents immigrated to the States because my father, as a worker in those days could not advance in his homeland. If you were in one class, you could not get out of it, so you would just have to be a poor worker all your life. So my grandparents, who were in the United States, saw that we got to the States.

"They lived in the Gallatin Valley in Montana. It was a huge Dutch settlement when we arrived there. I had one little brother and three sisters. It was about the time of the depression, 1930, a very, very poor time. It was a farm settlement with a few little stores and towns here and there, but otherwise they were all farmers raising potatoes and peas. My father worked for a farmer for a while, but pretty soon he had his own farm.

"There was a large Christian school, but I went to a country school. We had to walk about two miles, or a mile and a half, in the cold, cold winters."

Hattie explained that she got to know Egbert Dyk, "Because his folks were one of the families in the valley. I knew his sisters. There were at least one hundred or one hundred and fifty young people in the valley. Egbert's parents went to the Christian and Missionary Alliance Church and I went to Grace Bible Church.

"At our place, the Bible was read at every meal. We sat down to eat, and we prayed, we ate, the Bible came out and a chapter was read. We started at Genesis and ended at Revelation a year and a half later. So you had a real respect and awe for God. You knew there was a God. You knew what was coming. We didn't just read Bible stories--a nice story about this and a nice story about that--Daniel in the lions' den and a few others. You read the whole Bible. Hearing some stories, I used to get so mad at some of the kings that didn't follow the Lord. You lived with the stories and came to know all the doctrines of the Bible. You know the Lord is coming back. You know there is a heaven and a hell. You know all this. This is a real heritage.

"In the southern part of Holland, this is the custom: You don't just get up from the table and walk off. You don't say, 'May I be excused?' and leave the table. Often there are shelves under the table where they keep the Bible. The Bible comes out and they close with prayer. That's part of it. I think that's a great, great heritage.

"I think I was four years old when I started to pray that the Lord would save me because I didn't want to go to hell, and I wasn't good enough for heaven. I knew that. So I prayed as I was sitting on the bed when I was about four years old. My mother wanted to know what was wrong, and I said that I was praying that the Lord would save me.

"I always wanted to know the Lord, because I came from the Dutch background that believed you don't accept the Lord. That's not the issue. The question is, does God accept you? So for years I prayed that the Lord would accept me.

"I remember going to church one day and the minister said after he preached the sermon, 'Now a word to the unconverted.' "So I listened, and he said, 'Ye must be born again.' "And I thought, 'Well, I know that, but why don't you tell us how?' But that was not what they specialized in, the telling how. So there was the one night when He showed me, 'It's finished. Only believe.'

"Well, I knew then that the Lord had accepted me. The idea of evangelism, trying to get people to accept the Lord, does not go with people of that background. It's not 'Do I accept the Lord?' It's 'Does God accept me?'

"Many, many people have come to know the Lord in the Dutch settlement. There's a Christian radio station in the valley now, lots of churches, and a lot of Christians. So many cousins are Christians and go to Christian schools and to Calvin College in Grand Rapids.

"I was eighteen when I came to know the Lord and right at that time Mr. Maxwell of Prairie Bible Institute (PBI) [in Three Hills, Alberta, Canada] came to Bozeman, and he gave the message, a wonderful message. I still remember what he said: 'All things are yours, all things are yours,' which changed my life. This takes care of any inferiority complex because everything belongs to us. This changed my life completely.

"Then in a year or so I went to the Prairie Bible Institute for four winters and graduated in 1942. In my second year at PBI, Egbert showed up at PBI too. Dave Hart was on his way there, so he brought Egbert along.

"Egbert graduated in 1943. He went straight to the mission field in Mexico. I graduated in 1942. Then I worked in the Rocky Mountain Faith Mission in Montana for a little over two years, holding children's Bible classes in my home and preaching on Sundays in a little country church.

"I was going to continue working with the Rocky Mountain Faith Mission, but they wanted something from me. I've forgotten what they wanted, but I had to give an answer. They had to have an answer right away, but I wanted to be sure that I decided the right thing because I didn't want to make the wrong decision. So I went upstairs, and I prayed and asked the Lord to show me what I should say. Then I went downstairs and went upstairs again to pray because I couldn't get away from it. When I went up the third time to pray, I seemed to hear a voice telling me I would marry Egbert.

"And I thought, 'Well, that's not what I'm praying about.' I had to have an answer for the Rocky Mountain Faith Mission. So I skipped it and made the decision, whatever it was. And I didn't think much about what the Lord had said. In fact, I didn't know whether it was the Lord. Then, later on, slowly over time, I realized that it was the Lord who had given me his vision.

"But I stayed working in Montana, and I didn't even know where Egbert was. I decided, 'If this is what You're doing, Lord, You will have to do all of it. You'll have to take care of it every which way. I'll do absolutely nothing.' So I didn't. I continued working in Montana for a couple of years, I think.

"In 1944 I went to Summer Institute of Linguistics (SIL), as I felt that I should go into Bible translation work. Bob Schneider had sent me some literature, so I went and took the course at SIL.

"Then you had to have $100, and I didn't have any money. Working for the mission, I never got a cent. One day somebody invited me for coffee, and on the table was a $5.00 bill. I thought, 'Oh, my, you shouldn't give me that.' And under the $5.00 was $45! That was $50, and someone else gave me $50, so I had the $100. So I knew I was supposed to go to SIL. It was in Muskogee, Oklahoma, that year.

"After SIL I went back to Montana and went to PBI for a post-graduate course. The next year, my folks wanted me to stay home, but I wanted to go back to SIL. Then Dick Pittman asked me, 'Why don't you come in August and take the end of the course and then go straight to Mexico?' So that's what I did. That was 1945. A whole bunch of us went down to Mexico."

During those war years, while some American young men had been exempted from military service for one reason or another, most had been sent off to serve their country. This explains, at least in part, the imbalance of young men and women in Wycliffe personnel serving the Lord in Mexico at that time, which Hattie referred to next. However, another reason may have been that in the preceding years, many people had gotten the notion that missionary work was for women only, and young men were just beginning to recognize the challenge of going to unreached people.

Hattie continued, "The Lord was working it all out. One time, while I was at SIL, someone was talking about Mexico--forty single girls and Egbert was the only single man! Then somebody said, 'Oh, and he's engaged to such a nice girl.' And I thought, 'Well, You've got something else to work on, Lord.' I thought, 'That's all right. That's the Lord's problem. He'll have to take care of that.' And He did.

"Egbert broke up with this girl evidently. The funny part of it was that two couples in Mexico were so upset about it that they spent the whole night praying that Egbert would go back to that girl. Oh, dear."

Asked about her call to missions, Hattie replied, "It's the only thing to do. If the Lord chooses you, if the Lord picks you, if you come to know the Lord, then the only thing to do is to serve the Lord. There's no problem. It's not 'What do I want to do? What do I choose?' It has never been a matter of me choosing. It has always been a matter of asking the Lord what He wanted me to do."

Hattie did attend the first Jungle Camp session which started in southern Mexico in the fall of 1945. She was one of several single girls. Another was Elaine Mielke. She remembers that Titus and Florence Nickel were also among the campers. There were about twenty of them in all.

Hattie says, "Egbert had been down there before. He was what they called a field man. He was sent here and there to different tribes to help them until the summer of 1946. He and Uncle Cam bought the property for Jungle Camp, and Egbert and some of the others had been down there to build some huts. Then Egbert went to the States because he had malaria."

At another occasion, speaking before a group of Wycliffe members and associates, Hattie told of some of her experiences at Jungle Camp. She said, "It was the first Jungle Camp. So what were we supposed to learn and do? Uncle Cam was the Director, and he was engaged to Elaine. Elaine taught Spanish--taught all of us Spanish. We had classes in how to build a fire, because some people didn't know how to build a fire, and how to light a Coleman lamp and a kerosene lantern--the kind they used in the olden days in the barn--that kind. They wanted us to learn to swim and to learn to paddle a dugout canoe. Also we had to learn to cook on a wood stove, and besides that we had Indian culture classes. The Indians that lived around there were Tzeltal Indians so we studied some Tzeltal. There were hikes to make because Uncle Cam wanted us all to get stronger. Sometimes we had to go through the river. And the big finish at the end of the time was called The Baer Trip--a twenty-five-mile hike, uphill for most of the two-day hike, to visit with Phil and Mary Baer who had begun to work with a group of very primitive Lancandon Indians."

Hattie continued, "By the time the Jungle Campers had to go back to the Base Camp in the spring, the leaders had made a deal with Mission Aviation Fellowship (MAF) to send down a plane that had two wings on either side--a Waco biplane--and Betty Greene was the pilot. So Betty Greene and another MAF pilot started flying the campers out to Tuxtla, and they would land at a rancher's airstrip because that was longer than ours.

"So they were sending campers out, planeload after planeload; and Betty said to me, 'Hattie, why don't you stay? I have to get this plane to Mexico City. You and I can go together to Mexico City.' I needed to go there as Uncle Cam decided that I should go to take care of the group house, Quetzalcoatl, called the Kettle, because Esther Pierson, who was taking care of it, had to go to the States.

"So I stayed in Jungle Camp while they flew all those campers out. After the last load, the pilot who helped Betty landed at the airstrip at El Real. At the end of the airstrip there had been a building, and one corner pole was still standing in the ground. The pilot didn't see it so when he got to the end, he turned the plane around to go the other way and hit the wing on the pole, and that was the end of the plane!

"Another plane was going over, saw what happened, and they landed and took Betty in to report the accident. That left me and this new pilot and Colin Delgaty. He was sent down to take care of Jungle Camp for the summer. So there were the three of us. We thought, 'Oh well, Betty reported the accident. They know we're here. They know Uncle Cam wants me to take care of the Kettle, so they'll come after us.' But they didn't. They left us to stay there and stay there. We would walk down the hill every day to turn the prop of that plane so it wouldn't rust, I guess.

"They didn't come after us, and then Colin got sick. He had a fever. He was sitting in bed wheezing. I didn't know what to do. He had a temperature of 104! What were we going to do with him?

"So finally I said to the pilot, 'Let's walk to the ranch--Don Pepe's ranch. Let's see what I can do with all the Spanish that Elaine has taught me.' The pilot didn't know any. So we walked over to the ranch, and we explained the situation. We asked if somebody could go to Ocosingo, which was a good day's journey on a mule, to see if a local plane could come after us because we had to get Colin out to a doctor.

"So we did, and we thought that the plane would come. But the plane didn't come. So there we were. Every day we would go to the river and wash a little bit of clothes so everything would be clean, and fix some lunch for poor old Colin. What were we going to do? So finally, one day a plane came, but it went over. But then pretty soon it turned around and came back and landed.

"The old folks might know what kind of plane it was that holds at least ten passengers, and there were only three in there, so Colin and I made five. (The MAF pilot had to stay with the damaged plane.)

"So the pilot took off and he flew us to Tuxtla. But when we asked him what the price was, he charged us for the whole flight! Well, we didn't have the money. I knew we had to take Colin on the Pan Am flight from Tuxtla to Mexico City because he couldn't go by bus. He was too sick. So we talked to this pilot. He had been a friend of Egbert. We said, 'Would you mind waiting? We have to go to Mexico City. We have some money. We'll send it to you.' So he was kind. He said, 'Okay,' so we got to Mexico City. Colin had pneumonia, pleurisy and asthma, but he got well. And we stayed in Mexico City.

"At the end of that first session of Jungle Camp, all those campers gathered in Mexico City and went with Uncle Cam and Elaine to Peru. That was when the first group went down there. They traveled by boat.

"But I stayed. I felt I shouldn't go. I felt the Lord didn't want me to go to Peru. I loved Jungle Camp, and I wanted to work there because I happened to know a lot of the skills they were trying to teach everybody. I came from the farm. We were immigrants, and we knew what it was to light a kerosene lantern and pump up a gasoline lantern and light a wood fire and haul water. We knew all about that. We knew how to ride a horse. I felt that I could be of some help there."

But for that summer, Hattie was assigned to stay in Mexico City and take care of the Kettle. That gray, cut-stone building with tall windows still bore signs of its former elegance when it was the Hotel Quetzalcoatl. A tall, metal gate opened onto a paved yard or patio, bordered on the right by a high wall. At the left, an attractive, wide cement staircase with a cement railing rose to an ample landing, then turned left up to the second floor long, glass-enclosed porch. Rooms opened onto this porch. At the front were offices and a living room which provided a pleasant space for group meetings.

On the ground floor, opening onto the patio, were other rooms, including one for the house manager at the front and the group dining room and kitchen at the rear.

Managing the Kettle included assigning apartments to members arriving from tribal locations or from the U.S. It meant providing meals for them and overseeing the Mexican woman hired to clean the rooms. Hattie as the manager would also have had the responsibility of answering the jangling bell at the gate and receiving deliveries.

At that time the kitchen had not yet been adequately furnished with a good, large stove. She described having to prepare a banquet for officials with only two kerosene stoves to cook on. She said she and her helpers sent out for roasted chickens and other food, but without adequate storage facilities, even this was difficult. "Horrible!" she said.

At the end of the summer, she was invited out to Lake Patzcuaro in the State of Michoacan for a rest and a change. It is a beautiful lake in the area where Tarascan Indians live. They use big butterfly-shaped nets to fish on the lake, so it is particularly picturesque. Max and Elizabeth Lathrop were studying the Tarascan language in one part of the area, while two sisters, who were nurses, were also learning the language. They lived on the far side of the lake and needed a boat for transportation. Hattie stayed with them for a couple of weeks and also visited the Lathrops for two or three days.

She says, "The girls had a boat, but something was wrong with it. Egbert had come back from the States and was with the Lathrops a ways down at the other part of the tribe. So they sent Egbert to Patzcuaro to fix the boat. He fixed it and he left, but in no time there was something wrong with the boat again. So Egbert had to come a second time to repair the boat."

"It was that fall at Lake Patzcuaro where he proposed to me. When Egbert proposed, I said 'Yes,' and he said, 'Don't you want to spend some time praying about it?' But I didn't see any sense praying about something I had known for four and a half years!"

She went on to say, "Then we went into Mexico City, and Dick Pittman wanted us to hurry up and get married because he wanted to send us to Jungle Camp. We waited six weeks."

In those days couples didn't go back home to get married or to make other visits, as funds were at a minimum. So they got married right there in Mexico, where a civil marriage is required, while a religious ceremony is optional. Couples wanting both usually have the religious ceremony right after the civil one, if possible.

Hattie and Egbert had their civil marriage on Thursday, October 31, 1946; but because of All Saints' Day, they could not be married in the church until the following Monday. Another Wycliffe couple, Wilbur and Evelyn Aulie, were married in the Balderas Methodist Church in Mexico City on Friday, and the flowers they had to decorate the church remained there for the Sunday services. Hattie and Egbert made use of the same flowers for their wedding on Monday.

Hattie says that the two ladies who had been praying so earnestly a few years earlier for Egbert to get back together with his former girlfriend, helped her get ready for the wedding. She borrowed Isabel Sinclair's wedding dress. She had two attendants and Peggy Pittman was her flower girl. She does not remember what color their dresses were but all were floor length. They all carried lovely bouquets. Wedding pictures show the young couple looking very handsome, Egbert a few inches taller than Hattie.

Egbert and Hattie had been assigned to serve on Jungle Camp staff, so they left for the southern state of Chiapas soon after their marriage. A new group of young people was arriving for the Jungle Camp session and was proceeding to the capital of Chiapas.

Hattie said, "We had no plane then, so we stayed in Tuxtla Guttierez and rented a plane and bought all kinds of stuff--beans and rice and who knows what all, and filled the plane, and flew it all to Jungle Camp, with campers, except that there wasn't room for Egbert and me.

"So we said, 'That's fine. We'll take another plane to Ocosingo, and then we'll go in by horseback.' But the pilot felt bad about that. We had just been married and this was our honeymoon. He said, 'No, you've just been married. I don't want your wife to go overland. I have enough room on this plane--enough margin. I'll take your wife into Jungle Camp.'

"For public relations you do a lot of things. So for public relations I flew to Jungle Camp and left Egbert in Tuxla. Some people were already at camp.

"And guess what? The next day a *norte* set in. Do you know what a *norte* is? It's a wind from the north, and it's cold, and no plane flies when there's a *norte*. So there we were. I was in Jungle Camp; Egbert was in Tuxtla--no radio, no letters, no nothing, of course.

"Two weeks later Egbert came walking over. He had flown to Ocosingo somehow when the weather had cleared. And he came walking in. That was our honeymoon at Jungle Camp.

"Well, we had a good session. We did all the things we were supposed to do."

Hattie says that a medical doctor came down to help at Jungle Camp, and he was the Director. He and his wife and a few others made up the staff. Besides teaching classes to the jungle campers, they also took care of the needs of the Tzeltal Indians who came, buying from them tortillas and eggs and whatever they had to offer, and selling them soap and other simple things, and helping with their medical needs.

As she tells this, Hattie is speaking to a group of seniors-- Wycliffe members and associates at JAARS (Jungle Aviation and Radio Service)--and she addresses Elaine Townsend directly as she refers to Elaine's first baby, Grace, who had been born in Peru.

"And then, after Christmas--it was January, I think, Elaine. By that time little Gracie had been born, and little baby Grace came to visit Jungle Camp. So they stayed for a little while.

"They had flown in on one of those little Piper Cubs or whatever you call them--a commercial plane from Tuxtla. And they had made arrangements with the pilot. They said, 'Will you come and pick us up on such and such a date?' The pilot did. The pilot came and picked them up, and all of us were standing at the little airstrip over there to say goodbye. Don Pepe, the rancher, was with us.

"And I remember thinking, 'Boy, they have a lot going into that little plane,' and the pilot never weighed anything--didn't have any scales--no seat belts. So in they went and the plane took off. I can still see it taking off. It started off and then it started to wobble. And someone said, 'What's happening? What's happening?'

"And instead of landing--he could have landed in the pasture somewhere, though it would have been rough--but at least he could have landed--he decided to turn back to see if he could get back to the airstrip. So he started to turn back, but the tail hit a tree and there was a ravine there. The plane went for the ravine and jumped over.

"There was a little hill in front of where we were, so we all started running to see what happened. And there was Uncle Cam already lying in the grass with that huge cut in his hip. There was Elaine with a broken ankle, and somebody had the baby. And Uncle Cam was saying, 'Get away from the plane. Get the pilot out and get away,' because Uncle Cam was afraid the plane would blow up.

"So the men got the pilot. He was pushed against the dashboard or whatever you call it. They got him out, and then we all started to work. I still remember--nobody was there to say, 'You do this, you do that, you do that.' We just all pitched in. I picked up the baby. I took care of Gracie for three weeks. One of the ladies said, 'I'll take care of the food.' She went to the kitchen and took care of this and that. And the fellows went and cut poles and made stretchers. I don't know whether they had rope or sheets or what they used, but anyway they made stretchers and carried Uncle Cam and Elaine to a bedroom in one of the huts at Jungle Camp. And they were there for some time.

"The company that owned the plane sent in another plane. They took the pilot out and he recovered, but about two years later he committed suicide over a love affair. That was a sad story about that pilot.

"That accident was one of the reasons Uncle Cam decided we should organize JAARS to have our own planes and our own pilots who knew what they were doing, and we could count on them. There were other reasons also, but that was one of the reasons--that flight accident over there at Jungle Camp.

"So that was Session Number Two. As the years went by we had bigger sessions. The session that Marge Bancroft was in was a really small one. She was in the session with Rachel Saint, Marge Bondurant, Al Townsend and somebody else--a very small session. But the sessions increased. We had more and more. We built a clinic, and we improved.

"You know how you do when you improve things. Well, we improved it so much that Uncle Cam and others decided we needed an Advance Base, because we were getting too luxurious there. Anyway, it was decided we should have an Advance Base. They would pick out a site along a river somewhere, and then the campers had to build their own huts. They had to build their own stoves and all this kind of stuff. They got some help. But that was what Advance Base was for, because we had made it too good at the Main Base."

Hattie and Egbert were on staff at Jungle Camp for twenty-four years, from the fall of 1946 to December, 1970. Their three daughters were born in Mexico.

During this time the Mexico Branch established a children's home in Oklahoma City, so that their school-age children would be able to attend school in the United States while their parents continued working in Mexico. Hattie said, "When we went on furlough, they asked us if we would take care of the children's home, so we spent four winters in Oklahoma City."

After Hattie had served in the Mexico Branch for twenty-five years, and Egbert for twenty-seven, the directors sent them to Surinam on the north coast of South America, where several young Wycliffe members had already started learning the unwritten languages of that country and had begun Bible translation for them. Egbert and Hattie were sent there mainly because they could be of help to the Branch because they spoke Dutch, the trade language of that country.

"We went to Surinam in January, 1971. In Surinam, Egbert was the printer. I was the finance person, the bookkeeper, the treasurer, and everything. I was all alone, and I did it all by hand. We were there twenty-three years."

In January, 1994 they retired and moved into an apartment for retired Wycliffe personnel at the JAARS Center at Waxhaw,

North Carolina. Though retired, they volunteered their time, as many others do, so while he was able, Egbert helped in the print shop, while Hattie worked in the Purchasing and Shipping Department. Egbert died June 10, 2001.

"Egbert was real sweet. I remember him saying several times in his last days, 'I don't know how come the Lord was so good to give you to me.' Several times he said that. Fifty-four-and-one-half years we were married. It would be fifty-five November 4."

Hattie died on May 9, 2014 in Kirkland, Washington, at the age of ninety five. At her request, she was buried in Waxhaw, North Carolina, with her husband after a memorial service at the JAARS Townsend Center.

"Dear Lord, Please Give Jan A Husband. She Needs One."

" *I* was a teenage rebel," says Jan Townsend. "It was in a wonderful Christian home that I rebelled against--terribly rebelled against. My brother and my sister--all of us rebelled. My parents were very strict!"

Graduating from high school in 1938 at age sixteen, Jan left home immediately to find freedom. "I got a job with my cousin as a dental assistant, which I really liked. I didn't ever think I'd want to be a nurse until then," she recalled.

As a charter member in her parents' church, she always attended services when she was at home. "Because Mom thought I was a Christian," Jan said, "and I didn't let her know any different, she never knew what my life was like."

"At seventeen the Lord got through to me. Actually, I heard the same message I heard all my life, but it got to me. I mean, it became personal. God really changed my life."

Two young evangelists came to church at that time, but it was in her own room that she accepted the Lord. "That's when I heard about the Bible Institute of Los Angeles (BIOLA). I didn't know there was such a place." To her mother's dismay, Jan gave up a four-year scholarship at Redlands University to enroll at BIOLA.

A mission conference on campus dispelled her notion that missionaries were just stuffy old women. Several members of various mission organizations were present, but she was especially impressed by a missionary doctor, because she knew he could have been making good money somewhere else.

The Lord spoke to her she remembers, and she said, "I just about ran up the aisle. Very definitely, the Lord had spoken to me about going to the mission field."

After completing four years at BIOLA, Jan entered nurses training and completed the three-year course. After a year working with missions to migrant workers, she attended the Summer Institute of Linguistics (SIL) at Norman, Oklahoma, the following summer.

While at Norman, she filled out an application to join Wycliffe Bible Translators and began preparations to attend Jungle Camp and to go on to Peru. "Then I got cold feet and thought I needed to get some more nursing practice. So I put my application in my suitcase and accepted a job at Los Angeles County Hospital in the emergency department. It was a huge hospital even then, and the nurses in emergency were just awful, hard and really bad people. Later I found out some were also part of a drug ring. The Navigators, members of a Christian mission, led one of the girls to be saved. Bonnie, who lived in the same building as we, pulled out from the group and was raped and severely beaten several times after that, being persecuted because of her belief in Christ. One night she came to our apartment with a severe cut on her head. My roommate, a nursing instructor, treated her because Bonnie refused to go to the hospital since she knew the law required that the injury be reported to her family. Eventually, after continuing threats from gang members, she was moved to a mission safe house in Oregon where she died as a result of repeated blows to the head. But she never gave up her faith!"

"I was miserable because I knew I wasn't doing what the Lord wanted me to do. He had shown me that I was making the right decision with plans to go to Peru, but I was not willing to obey yet. One day my roommate said to me, 'Why don't you get going to where you're supposed to be?' I must have been miserable to look at, because I was miserable inside. I knew I wasn't doing what the Lord wanted me to do.

"So I got my application out again and called Mr. Nyman, who was secretary-treasurer of Wycliffe, and asked if he could help. He met me at the door with a screaming baby in his arms and said, 'Here, will you please do something with this baby!' His wife and daughter had gone shopping and had left him with a tiny granddaughter. He hadn't been with a tiny baby for twenty years or more, and the baby was screaming her head off. So I got her diaper changed, gave her a bottle, and I've often wondered if that may have gotten me into Wycliffe.

"The next day I gave my resignation to my head nurse. She just kind of sneered and said, 'You can't do this. You have to give a two-week notice.' I asked if she would be so kind as to give it to the nursing director. Later I was called to the director's office, whom I had never seen before because one just didn't meet the '*head honcho*.' She was a huge woman, sitting behind this huge desk, and gruffly invited me to sit down. I kind of gulped and sat down, while she sat there and didn't say anything for what seemed like hours. When she finally did speak, she was all choked up and said, 'I called you here to encourage you to do what you planned to do. When I was younger, I was going to go to the mission field, and I turned my back on the Lord, and I've had a miserable life.'

"So I got to leave, walk out of that office, walk down past all the staff in our department to say, 'So long!' They were just standing there with their mouths open.

"Some of the girls I knew gave me a shower of some of the things I needed for Jungle Camp. At the Army Surplus Store I got a jungle hammock and other things that were required gear. Then I took a trip from Los Angeles up to Oakland to see my mom and my church to bid them goodbye."

During the visit at church, Jan said, "A dear little old man was asked to pray for me. As he prayed he said, 'And dear Lord, please give Jan a husband. She needs one.' I just wanted the floor to open up and swallow me. It was so embarrassing--but his prayer was answered!"

"The next morning I went back to Los Angeles and on to Jungle Camp. I'll never forget the train ride with the Overholts, Earl Adams, and Doris Cox. We were the first group to get to Jungle Camp that season. I'll never forget feeling the peace that I experienced, knowing that I was going where I was supposed to go. I hadn't had peace for a long time, not since I left Norman with much hesitation about entering foreign missions. That was in 1947.

"I loved Jungle Camp. It was like a big vacation to me because I grew up in the country. Adele Malmstrom, Uncle Cam's niece, was with us. She thought we were invaluable to her because she had never lived in a primitive situation like that.

"Before I left Jungle Camp, I had a little session with the Lord about not wanting to go to the field as a single woman. I remember staying in my cabin almost the whole day reading, praying and crying, till finally I came to the place to say, 'Okay, I am willing to go without a husband. Okay, God!'

"After Jungle Camp I went back to Norman for my second year of SIL training. Sitting across the table from Al Townsend one day, I fell--flatter than a pancake! They say you don't fall in love at first sight, but I have a big argument with that, and so did Al. Our common connections were Mary and Phil Baer. Al had known them at Moody Bible Institute, and I had been out to their place at Jungle Camp. So, that's what we talked about mainly-- Phil and Mary!

"All summer long I waited for him to ask me out, but it didn't happen--and it didn't happen! Finally, it was the last week of school and something had to happen! The SIL staff took pictures of all students and staff that had been in Mexico in their colorful embroidered Indian outfits. I went over that afternoon and thought maybe Al will be there, and maybe if I leave early, he'll leave too and that's what happened. I left early, and he followed me and asked me to go with him to Oklahoma City the next day, which was Sunday. We had breakfast, went to church, enjoyed dinner and walked around the park before we had supper. It was quite a day!

"By then all the girls in the dorm knew I liked someone, but nobody knew who. All summer long they called him 'IT.' As we would go past someplace, they would ask, 'Is IT in there?' and I'd say, 'Yes.' But they never guessed his name, because he lived in the dorm for married men who were at school without their wives. So they thought Al was married, particularly because he was older than most. One day when I got back from a date, someone asked, 'Has IT asked you?' I said, 'YES!'

"When Al came to pick me up the next day, all the windows were covered with faces, looking to see who IT was, because they didn't know yet. That was quite an exciting week; it was final exam week, and I didn't do too well with that.

"Al and I met when I was already a Wycliffe member, and he knew that God had directed me in a certain way. He was not a member yet, and that was the reason he didn't ask me out earlier. He wasn't about to interfere with the call of the Lord on my life until he knew that he too would be a Wycliffe member. As soon as he knew he would be accepted in membership, he asked me for a date."

After graduation, Al went with Jan to visit her mother and her church. But before going to California, they made a detour to Louisiana for a week, so Jan could observe care and treatment at the leprosarium at Carville, the institution her great uncle founded. Jan said, "When we got on the bus on the hottest August day of that year, the air conditioning broke, and then someone threw up. It was awful and we could hardly wait to get to California to get a shower."

"When Al met my mom, he hadn't proposed yet, but I knew he was going to. He had to go to Jungle Camp yet, so he was headed for Mexico, and I was going to Peru.

"A funny thing happened when we went to church. Al was living out of a suitcase. We were sitting in church, my mother between us, and all of a sudden I saw her giggling. She pointed to Al's coat pocket, and there was his toothbrush sticking out. He had brushed his teeth and stuck it in there while he combed his hair or something like that.

"A friend of mine who had just married and was going to Africa asked if I knew someone who might want her wedding dress. Obviously I knew somebody! I tried it on, and there was not one thing that had to be altered. It fit perfectly, so I took it with me to Peru, even though Al had not proposed. It was about two letters after I got to Peru that he got on with it and proposed. My mother was a little upset with him because he didn't commit himself before I left.

"My friends had planned a party for me on Valentine's Day, but Adele Malmstrom died suddenly, so my party was cancelled. But Al's friend had a party for him at the Jungle Camp--an engagement party!"

During her time in Peru, Ellen Ross and Jan were allocated to the Machiguengas tribe. Ellen had gone there the year before by canoe. It took her twenty-seven days to get there. On this trip, the pilot, Larry Montgomery, flew them out in the first JAARS (Jungle Aviation and Radio Service) plane, the old Grumman Duck, which could land on the rivers in the midst of the jungle.

"Mr. Crowell, President of the Quaker Oats Company, and Mr. Robinson from Moody Bible Institute, who were on an orientation tour of translation sites, were on our flight that day. We landed in the area of the Piros tribe to visit Esther Matteson, the local translator, and where we spent the night. While there, Mr. Crowell noticed that Esther had a number of Quaker Oats containers lined up on a shelf. These were made of cardboard with very flimsy tops. She used them for storage. As she poured some sugar we brought in these containers, Mr. Crowell noticed that the lids were not very tight and ants could get in. After he got home, he designed a container that had a bigger top that fit down over the can. So he actually designed it so that missionaries would have better cans to store their provisions!

"Ellen and I continued the flight the next day to Timpia, the Machiguengas tribe area. The belly of the plane was cargo space, and the pilot and co-pilot were up above in a canopy." She remembered, "While flying over the rivers and jungle, I would just look down and praise the Lord. It took us two-and-a-half hours to get over the same terrain that took Ellen so long to travel."

"On arrival at Timpia," Jan continued, "we found out that there had been a flash flood. The river was just roaring down, and we remembered that before we left, Larry had worried about landing there. Then we realized that he actually wasn't able to land. He was taking off again! So we prayed fervently, and on the second attempt closer to the beach he was able to land and to tie up the plane. But the river was just a torrent of logs and all kinds of stuff. The pilot put a long rope--a long, long rope--on the plane and instructed some Indians to watch it all night so that as the river began to go down, it would let the plane go down with it and not get left way up on the beach.

"The next morning the Indians came sauntering back. Ellen could speak the language and asked them, 'How did the night go?' and they said, 'Fine, the plane is all gone except the tail.' Well, the pilot and the co-pilot ran down the path--I mean they ran as fast as they could! But the plane wasn't all gone. One half was under the roaring water, and they spent hours diving to secure it with ropes. Then they got all of the villagers to help to pull it back up. After hours of getting the mud and water out of the wings and getting it patched, they were able to take off again by the end of the afternoon. Before leaving, they told us they could never risk landing there again--it was simply too dangerous.

"And that was my first time out! I looked around at those people. I had never been anywhere like this before. I wondered if they would ever become personalities to me because they all looked alike. They all had gunny-sack dresses and had long hair with bangs. The women had babies strapped around their waists, so I knew they were women, but I couldn't really tell who were men and who were women until they began to *'get'* their personalities. It didn't take long before I realized that they all had painted themselves with colorful stripes, and that the men's stripes went up and down and the women's stripes went around. I also found out quickly that they were really a loving and fun people to be with.

"We had a little thatched-roof house with dirt floor, cooked over an open fire, and washed our clothes in the river. I loved it at the village. We lived on a point with rivers around us. From that point we could overlook the rivers and the sunsets which were absolutely beautiful. As the sun would go down, the rivers would look like black satin, and the jungle looked like black velvet. I had never seen sunsets like that before!

"The next challenge was diminishing supplies. Since the plane could not come back again, our supplies could not come either. We had a lot of Quaker Oats that Ellen had left on her last village stay, and we had some canned butter and a few staples like rice. But we knew we were not going to get the supplies that were to be coming up later!

"We did have a two-way radio. It was a great big, old Russian tank set. We could contact the Base and get help from doctors who would assist with diagnosis if someone was sick, and we could order additional supplies. But we were out just two weeks when our radio broke. I studied the maintenance manual like you would not believe, trying to figure out what was wrong so I could get it started again. I could just hear the JAARS guys back at the Base saying, 'Women, they won't know how to take care of anything.'

But after I gave the radio a shot of gasoline in the carburetor with a hypodermic syringe, it worked again!

"For three months we had no physical contact with the outside world. During that time Ellen worked very, very hard on the language to get it analyzed and reduced to writing, because she planned at the end of that year to go somewhere to evangelize and preach, and that wasn't part of our work. So while Ellen worked on the translation, I did all the cooking, the washing, and the medical work.

"The villagers were terribly afraid to come to us for anything medical, because they thought all white people were like the Spaniards who had been there before, had exploited them terribly, and had been very mean. How did they know those little white pills weren't poison?

"But one day Blanco came. He had a big swollen leg from a machete cut. It was badly infected, and he finally decided to let us work on it. We had some antibiotics, got it cleaned up, and he got well very fast. And that began to give the people a little bit of confidence.

"Along with him came a young man who had yaws, a tropical skin disease. His body was covered with sores from top to bottom. We had the medicine he needed, Ellen explained to him. She showed him the syringe and the needles and tried to assure him that a shot in the arm would make him get better. Well, he took one look at the syringe and needle and he was gone! He would come for days and Ellen would talk to him, but he would leave as soon as she talked about the shot. But one day he came and said he was ready. He wanted me to give him the shot. I can tell you, I prayed that the shot would go right into the vein the first time so I wouldn't have to poke for an entry. He was standing there with his arm out, he was shaking, and I was shaking! But with prayer, the needle went right in. When I finished, I had to tap him on the shoulder because he had his eyes closed and didn't even know it was over. He looked at his arm, he looked at me, and just took off whooping and hollering all around the village. He thought he had gotten up enough nerve for me to make a hole in his arm big enough to put the whole syringe in. When he saw that it was just a little bee sting, he got better really fast and came back every day for his treatments. After that the villagers began to come with their problems, and the medical work really took hold.

"One day the Indians came running and saying, 'There's a plane coming!' They could hear it long before we could. I don't know that you could possibly understand how exciting that was, knowing that a plane was coming after three months of extreme isolation.

"It was a little plane on wheels--the little Aeronca which is hanging up in the hangar at JAARS even now. It couldn't land, but it dropped our mail, and the pilot did a great job of making it land right in front of our house and not in the river. Right on top was a note that said Al had just arrived in Peru, and a plane was to come out to get me, and we were to be married! There were about a dozen letters, but someone else had written the note that he had just arrived.

"Another radio was also sent out from Base Camp, but it took another two weeks for us to get it. One night we heard this cow horn down river and realized that a boat was coming. We quickly finished our supper, got ready to set the radio up, and I knew I could talk to my sweetheart for the first time in a year--with the whole world listening to our sweet nothings. We started calling, and we called for forty-five minutes, but got no answer. Finally it crackled on, and we heard someone on Base say that they had gotten our first call, but their transmitter was out and they were madly trying to get it fixed.

"When Al and I finally talked, we started to make wedding plans. We talked every day after that and decided on a date without knowing when a plane was going to come to get us. Our radio went out again! This time it was something I could not fix, and it made me feel better to know that it wasn't something we were too stupid to know how to repair.

"It would be another three months of waiting for that plane to come. In the meantime everything sounded like a plane coming: the bees flying, the pigs over the hill, everything sounded like the plane coming!

"One day Ellen and I were down at the river. We had just washed our hair when she said it was time for the plane to come. Just then we heard the plane. This was a bigger plane. There were seventy-two muddy steps up that bank, and I think the Lord put wings on me. I made it up to the cabin in two seconds--just went flying up those steps, waving as the plane flew over. Al was in the plane! As the plane flew over, I thought Al probably looked down and wondered, 'What did I promise myself to do?' My hair was flying, and I was wearing my old moldy housecoat and my bathing suit.

"The plane couldn't land, but they dropped a note to see if we were okay, or if they needed to make an emergency landing. We didn't need that. We were instructed to go three days down river by canoe to a place where they could land. Then they flew around again and dropped another note, which we did not find. We were eager to start packing so we could get ready to leave early in the morning. When we got to the river the next day, we found the note that said another package drop had 99 letters for me. Al had counted them and put them in the packet. That packet is still out in the jungle somewhere, but I was going back to Base Camp to get my m-a-l-e!!

"On the last day of the three-day-canoe trip, knowing that around the bend was to be the plane and my sweetheart whom I hadn't seen for a year, I was so excited while combing my hair and powdering my nose! But around the bend there was no plane. We got off the river not knowing where they had landed or when they would be coming. We found a little stream down a little ways that would be a good place to take a bath, and while we were skinny dipping, there came the plane! Obviously we dressed very quickly.

"The Grumman Duck is amphibian. It can land on the water or on land. It did land on water, but then it just kind of walked up to the shore, at least that is the way it looked on wheels.

"Al and I met at the *Playa No Me Olvides* which means Forget-Me-Not Beach. Later, sitting on duffle bags in the cargo area of the plane, Al and I were making up for lost time while flying over the jungle, and I got my engagement ring! We had not seen each other for a year. When we got to the new Jungle Base at Yarinacocha, I found out that Al had been there for three months while I was with the tribe trying to get out.

"Al had been allocated to help establish the new Base. There was no road into the town near this new site, so they had to bring in everything by canoe--lumber, bricks, and all building materials. They finally got an old Burma Jeep, and Al and the guys built a road into town. That was some road! When it rained, it was just one big mud puddle--red clay which caused the jeep to slip and slide. But it was a road, and they could bring in supplies.

"As we were walking up the hill, Al said, 'There is our house.' I thought we would have to live in group housing, but he had made this little cracker box for our home. It had two rooms, a thatched roof and screens around the whole outside. The unbleached muslin ceiling kept bugs, rats and other pests from falling into the rooms while we were sleeping. And it was wonderful! The house was not quite finished, and Al wanted to get all the work done before we went to Lima to get married. I went to the house to '*help*,' but all we did was stand behind the screen and smooch.

"At a wedding shower, the few people who were there gave us rare gifts: a can of stateside peaches which were so expensive that four people got together to buy it, a can opener, a Shipibo pottery bowl, and one other item I can't remember. That was it. When I thought of showers at home, just loaded with everything,

I realized that we had just as much fun. We really didn't need very much to have fun and be happy."

Jan and Al planned to have a religious wedding on the day after the civil ceremony, just in case the papers weren't ready, which is exactly what happened. When they got to the civil office at City Hall, the papers were not available until the next day, so they ended up having both ceremonies on the same day. "I didn't know Spanish," Jan recalled, "and the guy who was our witness said for me to just say 'Si Senor' when he nudged me. I guess I said it at the right time, because we were married. The official who performed the civil ceremony was a little chubby Peruvian who gave me a beautiful bouquet of white flowers."

"Our real wedding ceremony was in a beautiful, beautiful Peruvian home in Lima. One of our mission couples was house-sitting for the owners. The home had a beautiful winding stairway that came down into the living room. We put loops of ribbon on the chairs and made it look like a wedding chapel with a fabric lining rolled out on the floor.

"Decorating until the last minute, I was still in pedal pushers (now known as capris) and curlers when the first guests arrived, and I looked just horrid. Rushing to get ready without my matron of honor, who was busy getting herself ready, I confronted some 40 buttons on my wedding dress all on my own, wondering if I would make it to the ceremony at all. Ralph Sandell acted as my dad. He was very nervous, and as we went down the staircase, he was shaking so much that the foil in the back of my bouquet was rattling all the way. I was holding him up instead of him holding me up. I had just one attendant, who wore a long, light green dress. I just didn't have any close friends in Lima.

"When Al came out of the kitchen to stand at the altar as I was walking down the aisle, he was munching on something! But it was a really nice ceremony. We had a pump organ which one of the girls played very nicely. Don Burns sang 'Together Forever,' a beautiful song I had not heard. We had memorized our vows and said them to each other."

Jan said they were married by the Christian Missionary Alliance pastor, and they had a very simple reception at the Peruvian's home. For their honeymoon, they went to the Missionary Alliance cottage up in the mountains above Lima.

"Larry Montgomery drove us to the cottage in Uncle Cam's old car, which normally took about an hour. He stopped three times to take a quick nap; he was so exhausted from a demanding flight schedule. That car is now in the Mexico-Cardenas Museum at the JAARS Center in Waxhaw, North Carolina.

"Our friends had told us that the cottage would not really be a good place for a honeymoon, but we felt that any place would be a good place as long as we were together. When we arrived there, we had a problem finding the key. When we got inside there was no water and the well was dry. An old ditch with water ran past the cabin, so Al got buckets of water for the bathtub, and we had chemicals to purify the water enough to boil it for drinking. Then we walked into the bedroom. Here were two camp cots! We stood there and just howled! We agreed that our friends knew what they were talking about when they said that this was not a good place for a honeymoon. But there were mattresses on those cots, so we put them on the floor. So much for our bedroom in the honeymoon cottage!

"We waited for the photographer until midnight. He had decided to go to the movie theater since we were late arriving at the cottage. His excuse was that he thought we might have had too much to drink to get there at the appointed time.

"It had gotten very cold by then, and as I walked to the window to close it, I doubled up with pain. My appendix was acting up. Al came to shut the window when it slipped and smashed his thumb. He was holding his thumb and I was holding my side. That was our wedding night!"

Jan and Al stayed at the cottage a few days, and finally someone took them to the American Clinic, but Jan didn't have surgery for a couple of days because she had a cold. Ending their honeymoon at the clinic, they took two single girls back to the honeymoon cottage. Jan recalled, "The girls came in from staying with a tribe and had experienced a very, very tense time. The Indians had been killers, and it was not a safe environment. Since friends in Lima kept asking them to relate the details, we invited them to come with us so that no one would know where to find them. Certainly nobody would think that we would take two single girls back up with us on our honeymoon, but there was plenty of room for all of us."

On the way back to the big Jungle Base at Yarinacocha, they flew from Lima over the Andes in a commercial plane to Pucallpa, and then bounced in an old ambulance over the road Al had helped construct.

Soon after this adventure, the first Peru Branch conference was held. This involved making changes to accommodate personnel coming back from their jungle allocations.

"Al put a partition up that created two rooms in our little house. We hosted three girls in one room, and we were in the other for the duration of the conference. Later we pulled the partitions back out, but it was fun to have guests in our new home. We were the first couple to have an ice cream freezer with an old hand crank. We could get ice from a gas-powered refrigerator and collect a lot of saw dust to bring it home. Of course, we had to wash off the ice to be able to chop it up. That was a lot of work, but we'd have the whole Base for ice cream until it began to get so big that we had to divide guests into two groups. Things were primitive, but we had really great times in those days.

"Al and Nick built the first big building on the new Base to house four families, two single girls, a small dining room with a kitchen, and even a small clinic. The partitions were sheets of aluminum so you could hear everything from the next room. Now that building is just a big dining room.

"When the Bondurants got married, the partitions in the building were removed to create one big room for the wedding. This was the first wedding at Jungle Base. The guys made a beautiful archway with ferns and branches. Everyone brought something to decorate: someone had a nice lace cloth; someone else had candles; and someone else had silverware. I made the wedding cake--the bottom layer in a pressure cooker, the next layer in a smaller pressure cooker, and the next one in just a little pot over the open fire. The powdered sugar we had was lumpy, so we grated it to make it powder again. It took forever to grate those lumps!"

An event that happened before Jan went to Peru made a significant difference in what Jan was able to do. She recalls, "One night, right after I graduated from nurses training and worked in the Women's and Children's Hospital in Los Angeles, I gave my roommate a Toni, a permanent hair curl. This turned out to be the most stupid thing I'd ever done. We didn't have gloves back then. The next day my fingers were swollen. My doctor informed me then that this was the end of my nursing career because I would never be able to sanitize my hands as nurses have to do. I cried and cried. And then when I got to my field assignment, I was exposed to a fungus. Coming back to the Base camp, I was assigned to the clinic but realized that I could not work there because I had eczema on my hands."

"So I was assigned to the kitchen for about a year. Talk about a challenge! We had a three-burner kerosene stove and a little tin oven to put over a burner. There was no refrigeration. We had sixty people to feed! You cook differently when it's like that. I started baking rolls and bread with yeast made out of sweet potatoes and some concoction the Indians used to ferment their drink. Making yeast was difficult, but oh, did that bread taste good. We had not had bread for so long that it was worth the challenge.

"We ate lots and lots and lots of pork, very little beef, and chicken was the most expensive meat to buy. The only fresh vegetables available were potatoes, onions, beans and cabbage. We did have some canned corn and peas. It is surprising how many ways you can use these to come up with different recipes. A favorite was cooked cabbage with bacon and peas.

"Pucallpa had about fifty residents and two stores that had everything, but the 'everything' wasn't a lot. Now it is a metropolis in comparison. There was one traffic light in our day and only one-way streets congested with three-wheel bikes. When it rained and planes came from Lima, they would often have to turn back because the airstrip was one sea of mud. Many times when we went to the airstrip, it was just to turn around because it started raining.

"We were married in 1949. A year and a half later I got pregnant, but I had dysentery and lost that baby. My husband was devastated. He just sobbed and sobbed because he wanted a child so badly.

"Then we went to Lima for Spanish study. It was my hope to get pregnant again there. We lived with a Peruvian family, and the father smoked those horrid smelling Peruvian cigarettes. The hostess assigned me a seat right next to the father, and soon I began to get sick to my stomach from the smoke. I would run to the bedroom and lose my supper, until one day the woman of the house said, 'I know what's the matter with you--you're pregnant.' And I was! That was Tim. I lost 30 pounds while I carried him, and having him in Lima was a nightmare."

Because there was not a full clinic at the Base, Jan and Al stayed in Lima. She had an American doctor, but Jan said, "He was Catholic; and they believe if there are childbirth problems, it is right to save the baby because the mother has already had her life. It was kind of a funny feeling knowing that."

"The doctor had a private practice and could admit patients to four different hospitals. He had me choose which one I wanted. I chose the Seventh Day Adventist because they said not to bring in anything from the outside since everything was sterile in their hospital. It was reassuring to know there was a clean place in a third-world country.

"We were at the Group House during lunch time. I was upstairs going through a trunk of stuff when I had my first hard pain. Then in twenty minutes a second one and every minute and a half after that. I wanted to go to the hospital and told Al. Marian Wacker was housemother at the time. She said, 'Oh for goodness sake let your husband eat his lunch. You've got twelve hours yet.' But I insisted and by the time we got to the doctor's office, I was half dilated and progressing fast. He called the Seventh Day Adventist, but they had four babies that morning and could not take me. Neither the German nor the Italian hospitals had any beds left! The only other place that would take his patient was a Peruvian hospital for the elite. When we told him that we could not afford that, he made some kind of arrangements because he could not deliver a baby in the office.

"This was June, and that is winter time in Lima. It's cold and foggy. There was no central heat anywhere. Peruvians don't heat their homes at all. When we got to the hospital, we found out that we had to bring everything! And we had nothing with us! Al went tearing home to get clothes for the baby. Going to the delivery room, I was placed stark naked on a gurney--just a sheet to cover me--and then they took that away to put me on the delivery table. It was like lying on a cake of ice! I was pretty shaky by then anyway, nervous, wondering if I was going to make it. Tim was born while Al was getting the clothes, so all there was to put around the baby coming out of that warm canal was a gauze diaper. The staff said that he almost died of the cold, but that is all they had to cover him.

"The hospital had a nice little living room from where visitors could see into the patient rooms. All of the visitors would sit in that little *sala* and talk to each other, but no one talked to Jan.

Families would come with maids and big bassinets. Although the hospital was for the elite, they too had to bring everything the patient needed, just like we did.

"It was a blessing to be at this elite hospital because my doctor was also in charge of the Peruvian Maternity Hospital downtown where the poor people went. It was said that they would have been better off staying at home to have their babies in their own germs. The hospital employed midwife staff from England who needed to gain experience before obtaining their licenses. The conditions at the Maternity Hospital were medieval! Two patients in labor usually occupied the same bed. Sheets were not changed between patients. Nurses had gloves to protect themselves, but they did not change them between patients. It was said that if patients did not have venereal disease when they were admitted, they did have it by the time they were discharged. Had my doctor not made special arrangements, I would have had to deliver Tim in that hospital!

"We signed out of the hospital and that day the sun shone. It had been overcast and cold for days, so it felt like leaving prison. Tim suffered from colic, cried day and night which kept us from getting sleep. But it was a new, blessed day for us and our first child, and the sun shone!

"Al had pursued the translation work for *'our'* tribe. He went out six different times to see if he could find the chief of this very nomadic group. Finally he did get permission for us to come to the village. When he came back from the survey trip, he said he had never seen gnats and bugs like that anywhere. Al built a type of playpen with fine mesh for Tim that would keep the bugs out and serve as his bed as well. Then he went back to the tribe to build a house for us. When the plane came back to get me, Al was in the plane. There had been a flu epidemic, and the Indians had died like flies from the flu. The chief had died. There was only one man left in the village. Everybody who survived had just scattered.

"When Uncle Cam heard that, he said, 'You have tried, really tried, to get out to these people, but now I want you to go to Ecuador on the Advance Team and get the first group house started. When you finish that, come back to the Base Camp as support personnel.' That was the end of our translation dream. I would never have made it as a translator because I found languages hard to learn. Al could have; he was a student. But I do think that we were much better in the support role. Al and Nick built most of the Base Camp as it grew.

"Two years later Judy was born in the clinic at the Center after only 45 minutes in labor. When she was six-weeks old, we went to Ecuador by boat, an Italian liner. On board, all the men were placed on one side of the boat, and the women and children on the other. Three of us had six-week-old babies. That was an unusual experience, but fun.

"In Quito every day was busy with searching newspapers and walking all over town to find a house big enough to serve as the first Group House. We got it set up, opened it for staff and had our first meal, inviting the Minister of Education. We hardly had enough silverware to go around. The Advance Team members were the first Wycliffe missionaries to be welcomed to Ecuador.

"We were in Ecuador just for three months when we went on our first furlough to visit our supporters and churches. We also went to Al's home to meet his ten brothers and sisters and his dad. I had not met any of them. They lived in Philadelphia, and it felt like going home to meet the Board of Directors.

"It had been cold in Ecuador. Tim had on a pretty little sweater; he was two-years old. When we got to Panama it was sweltering hot, and he would not take his sweater off. We had all cold-weather clothes with us in August, and it was hot. When we got to Miami and found a drugstore that had some clothes, I bought a cotton dress. Did it wrinkle! And the kids had an ice cream cone and got it all over me. So to meet Al's family, I looked like 'The Wreck of the Hesperus.'

"Back in Peru, two years later Barb was born. She was our strawberry blond. Judy was blond and Tim was a brunette. We had a full clinic in Peru by then, which was like heaven--efficient nurses and a doctor. It was wonderful after the nightmare in Lima to have a Christian doctor and Christian nurses!"

Though they were support personnel, Al and Jan spent some time in the Machiguenga tribe. Jan explained that Ellen had begun the work there, and then Wayne and Betty Snell took over. It was a different village from where Jan had first gone, but the same tribe; and they loved being with the tribe. They served there three different times as a family to help when there was sickness. She remembered well washing diapers for three small children--just gritting her teeth while doing so! The New Testament in that language was completed, and there is now a thriving church.

"We served there for four more years when our Patty was born six weeks before we went home for furlough," Jan said. "We remained in the U.S. to care for Patty, who lived for sixteen years with severe medical problems. During that time she was part of a developmental measles vaccine study. That vaccine eventually saved many Peruvian villagers from dying like flies during measles epidemics. So we were comforted to know that our Patty actually had a big part in our work in Peru."

Eventually, after many visits to dermatologists that did not resolve Jan's skin problems, she had a hysterectomy fifteen years after they came home. After that her hands healed, and the doctor explained that a hormone change in her body made the difference.

"We celebrated our 50th anniversary at our home assignment at the JAARS Center," Jan explained. "The kids staged one of these memory lane games and would ask me a question that Al had to answer. One of the questions was about the color of the bridesmaid's dress. He said, 'Green.' I couldn't believe that he would remember. All through the game he had the right answers. It was really amazing!"

The bond Jan and Al formed was obviously strong enough to overcome challenges, as well as support their love for each other.

After a period of active involvement at JAARS, they planned to move to a retirement village in the area. Al died before that happened. Jan made that move, where she found fellowship among Wycliffe colleagues and new friends. She went to be with the Lord after a few months there.

"We Have Your Tickets, But--"

*I*f anyone had suggested to Martha Duff, while she was growing up, that she would be living in the jungle most of her life, she probably would have said something like, "Me?-- Living in the jungle? You can't mean it!" If they had predicted that she would translate the Holy Scriptures for a tribe of Indians who had never seen their language written down, she most likely would have found that possibility even more unbelievable. She didn't even know the Bible very well in those first years.

When she was thirteen-years old, "Way back in my Methodist church in east Tennessee," she said, "I understood about Christ dying for me, so I decided that I wanted to believe that and follow Him, but it wasn't real to me."

A couple of years later, her family moved to Columbus, Ohio, where she learned more about the Christian life from Charles E. Fuller's radio program, 'The Old Fashioned Revival Hour.' One day he preached on Romans 12:1 (KJV), "I beseech you therefore, brethren, by the mercies of God, that you present your bodies a living sacrifice, holy, acceptable unto God, which is your reasonable service."

Martha said, "I realized that it was a challenge I couldn't get away from. I had to do something about it. I went to my room, knelt down and committed my life to the Lord for whatever He might want. When I made that commitment there in my bedroom, I thought right away that I wouldn't tell my parents, because nobody in our church or in my family has ever done anything like this. My parents will think that I'm a fanatic. They'll probably say, 'Oh, you don't want to do that,' or something like that. So I just didn't tell them, because this was real, and this was what I intended to do."

Martha immediately went out and bought a Bible and started reading it. She said, "I realized, boy, there's so much in there!"

After finishing high school, she took a short course in commercial subjects, got a job where she could make extra money working overtime, and started saving up for further training. For four years she worked and saved money, until she thought she might have enough to go four years to college.

Where would she go to school? The literature which came to her home from her church's denominational publishing house seemed quite liberal, so she did not want to go to any of the church colleges it represented. She wanted to find a school that taught the Word as Charles E. Fuller had taught on those radio programs.

"The only place I knew that might be something like I wanted would be Moody Bible Institute, maybe," said Martha. "So I wrote to them, but they were filled up and would be for many months.

"I had a boyfriend at that time. I told him what I was planning to do and what I really meant to do in the future so that I wouldn't be leading him on, but I also told him that I hadn't told my parents. When I was with him during this time, he would ask me, 'Have you told your parents yet?' And I'd say, 'No, I haven't gotten up my nerve yet, but I plan to.' I appreciated that, because it did force me to make that definite with my parents.

"So one night, as I came home from work, I determined that this would be the night to tell my mother. As I sat down with her, I just came out with it. 'I've decided I want to be a missionary.' My mother didn't say anything right away, which was unusual for her because she was quite a talker, always having something to say. My assumption was that she didn't like it, but then I realized that she probably thought I would tell her that I wanted to get married. And here I come out with, 'I'm going to be a missionary.'

"When she recovered from that, she said, 'Now if you're sure that's what God wants you to do, then when dad comes home from work we'll tell him, and we'll both support you in any way we can.' I was very happy about that and that I had their full support."

Then her mother suggested that they talk to a woman they had known when she was growing up, a fine Christian with whom the family always had devotions together. This woman had become a missionary to the Native Indians in the western United States and told Martha about Columbia Bible College in Columbia, South Carolina. Martha decided to attend that college, and on her first trip her boyfriend took her to the bus station where they decided they would make this their final goodbye.

About the Bible College, she said, "I didn't realize that there would be places like that where God's Word was taught in such a way that they based their lives on it. I had never seen that degree of commitment to anything. I was just enthralled as I got into those Bible classes, feeling as though I was getting so much of the Word so fast that I couldn't contain it all. I spent a wonderful four years there."

At Bible College she first heard about Wycliffe Bible Translators from Ethel Wallis. Martha remembered, "She taught us how to say potato without aspirating the 'p' and 't' sounds. She was really nice and I liked her, but thought I could not do that kind of work. I felt I didn't have enough brains to get into the linguistics work."

Although she didn't decide at that time to join Wycliffe, she decided that the linguistic training would be helpful for whatever she might do, so she and a girlfriend decided together to go to the University of Oklahoma where Wycliffe held the Summer Institute of Linguistics (SIL). That was in 1951, and she went directly to Oklahoma upon graduation from Bible College.

There she learned how to make all kinds of sounds that occur in languages around the world, how to recognize and to write these, and how to analyze grammars that are totally different from English. She was impressed that many of the teachers were Wycliffe members who had doctorates in different fields of linguistics.

And even though the courses were intensive, she realized that she was making average or above-average grades. Attending the orientation courses about the policies of Wycliffe, Martha especially liked the fact that Wycliffe encouraged indigenous work, which meant not going out as church builders, but as translators. "This meant working towards building an indigenous church rather than one that a missionary would establish," Martha realized. "So, despite the fact that I went to the SIL course not intending to apply to this mission, I wound up about midway through the course actually deciding to do just that! I prayed to God not to let me be accepted if this was not the right place for me, because I wasn't too sure how far I could go in linguistics. But I liked literacy also, another Wycliffe emphasis, and I knew that I could do that. So I made my application for Wycliffe membership, which was accepted."

"My first choice of assignment was Mexico because it seemed like a more logical place to work in literacy than a more remote assignment like the jungles of Peru. But as I got to Mexico, I was partnered with Ethel Wallis, a linguist, and she wanted me to stay and be her permanent partner. She was such a wonderful person, and I learned so much from her during the year or so I worked with her. The way Ethel worked with the Otomi Indians was a great help to me later on in my work.

"But while I was in Mexico, I decided that I really wanted to get into more pioneer mission work. At that time, the work was just opening up in the jungles of Peru, across the Andes Mountains, toward the interior of the continent of South America."

So Martha changed direction, settled on a linguistics career, and went directly from Mexico to Peru. She says her sister and her brother-in-law met her in Mexico and drove her around the Gulf of Mexico to Miami, stopping in New Orleans to ship her belongings from there. For the flight from Miami to Lima, Peru, she had the company of another Wycliffe friend, Viola Galensoski.

Wycliffe had an office in the Peruvian capital, Lima, but Martha didn't lose much time there, moving right out to Wycliffe's Jungle Base, Yarinacocha, where numerous dwellings occupied the bank of a beautiful jungle lake. Here Wycliffe maintained a large base of operations, including a hangar for JAARS (Jungle Aviation and Radio Service) planes to fly translators to the interior jungle locations where they worked.

Martha told how she and Mary Ruth Wise, who had been one of her classmates at Columbia Bible College, had decided to be partners. Since the work among the Amuesha Indians was just opening up, they were asked to consider going to that tribe. This was not long after she arrived in Peru, so she didn't have much time to think about it, but they were both willing to go wherever linguists were needed.

"So the day came that we were ready to go," she recalled. "That was a great day because, after all I'd been through in preparation, I could hardly believe that this is really it! I'm going to get in that JAARS plane and fly right out to a tribal group of people! High spirits prevailed; and we got all the duffle bags and six months of supplies and paper materials, books and everything that we would need, and finally got in that plane and got started! Jim Price was our pilot.

"As we flew out, we saw this beautiful rainbow in the sky. I don't know how, but the pilot maneuvered the plane into such a position that we could see this rainbow all around us. I remember thinking, 'Isn't this a beautiful thing that God gives us, like a rainbow of promise as we start!' But just a few minutes after leaving the Jungle Base, all you could see below the floats of the plane were deep jungle and rivers, and it did not look like anyone could live there. That is all we saw for almost two hours.

"Then I sensed that we were going down, and soon I could see this small river--a beautiful, clear river. I looked for a village or any habitation, but it looked like we were just about to land in the rapids. However, the pilot knew where to find a large enough pool of water in this small river coming down from the Andes Mountains--a safe place to land.

"But just about the time the floats splashed down into the water, I started to get second thoughts. As we were rushing down, splashing water up on both sides as float planes do, these second thoughts started rushing through my head just as fast as they could! I was thinking, 'Are these primitive people going to accept me? Will I be able to learn their unwritten language? Will I be able to live in this jungle all this time?' Just one question after another, and even though the plane slowed down, my thoughts didn't! I could feel my knees going just as weak as they could be.

"By this time we had come to a stop in the water, and the pilot turned to go back to the place where he wanted to dock. Just as he turned the plane around, I looked up from my position in the back seat, and there were all these Indian people lined up on the bank of the river, in single file because all wanted to get a front row view of this thing which they'd never seen before--people flying in an airplane and landing on the water! I think we were probably the first white people some of them had seen. This was a great happening for the Indians!

"So there they were, all lined up. I looked at them and saw that they wore dark, long, rustic tunic garments. They had long hair, and some of them had their faces painted red and some black. They looked fearsome--and that didn't help my knees at all--they just got weaker and weaker.

"Then, as the pilot turned toward the bank of the river, I had another very anxious thought. I realized that, 'I'm going to be the first one out of this airplane--the first one to have to walk out on the float and meet the people!' Because my partner, Mary Ruth, was sitting in the front seat of the airplane, and there was no door in the front of the plane, the door was on the back row of seats near me. And I knew that she would have to wait until the pilot got out and got the rope and threw it out, hoping that some of the people on the river bank would catch the rope and hold it to keep us from floating back down river before he could let her out. So that didn't help my knees either. They just continued to get weak as water, like that beautiful clear water I was looking at down below us.

"I watched anxiously as they got the plane tied up to a bush, and then I knew that the moment of truth had come for me. I opened the door on my side, and let's just say that I deliberately slid my body down from that seat, down till I felt my foot touching the float below. I got onto the float and took time to steady myself because the water was still in motion, so I had to get a steady grip to keep from falling into the water. So I started to walk the length of the float, out onto the beach where the people above were standing still. As I got my balance and started walking, I remember thinking, 'I wish that JAARS had made their floats a little bit longer because I'm going to get there too soon!'

"But in spite of all these uncertainties of whether the people would accept me and whether I'd be able to do this, of one thing I was really sure--that this was the place that God had for me. There was no doubt about that. So with even my little faith, I walked to the end of that float.

"And just as I got to the end of the float and took that big, giant step from the float onto Amuesha land, a wonderful thing happened! A young girl, about thirteen-years old, broke from the crowd of people on the high bank. She came down very quickly, and it seemed to me by the time my foot hit the ground, she was there. She took me by the hand. It wasn't a handshake, because the people didn't do handshakes. She just took me by the hand because she wanted to be friends with me--I could tell that right away. She started to look at my clothes, rubbing the material of my dress; and she started talking at full speed, and of course, I didn't understand a word of it. I heard her talking, but we were going into a monolingual situation, where the people only talk this language; and there had been no way for us to learn the language before being with the tribe. So you had to learn the language as you arrived.

"I had purposely worn this bright floral skirt since I had heard that Indians like bright colors, and she really liked this skirt. I heard her say again and again, '*go-o-win, ah-tash-go-o-win.*' So I thought this *go-o-win* word must mean something, and I hoped it meant 'pretty' or 'good.' I was to learn later that it not only meant 'pretty,' but it meant 'good.' It meant 'well.' It meant everything positive. So as I had scarcely left the JAARS plane, I learned one of the most important words that would be used in translation in years to come, because we had come to give the Good News--that same word--the Good News of the Gospel of Jesus Christ.

"By this time my partner and the pilot were coming up the shore, and we started going up the river bank. It was very slippery, and my little newfound friend was holding on to me. She didn't let go of my hand, for which I was very happy. My knees were getting a little bit better, but not too good yet; and then I saw this big old, black buzzard. As it swooped down over us, my little friend pointed to it and said, '*tsipm, tsipm,*' so I realized that she had given me the name of the buzzard. I quickly put that down in my memory--that a buzzard from henceforth and forevermore would be called a *tsipm*. We don't have the 'ts' sound in English, so if I hadn't learned that in my linguistic course, I wouldn't have been able to pronounce it the way she did. But I was able. In fact, I could see that word written in phonetic script as we had learned how to write sounds that we had never heard before.

"Having learned my first two words in Amuesha just as I got away from the JAARS plane, it seemed all so natural by this time that I didn't realize that God was already answering my questions of whether or not I'd be able to learn the language or if the people would accept me, because this little girl had already become my best friend, and she already taught me some of the language!

"The people lent the translation team an empty house. It had a thatch roof and walls made of strips of bark from palm trees. There were wide cracks between the bark strips, so the Indians could easily see through and watch every activity!

"That was our first culture shock," said Martha, "to realize that there was not going to be any more privacy. But that wasn't too bad, once we decided that we would not do anything we wanted to keep from anybody anyway. But it was still funny to see little eyes looking at us in our house through these cracks to see just what we were doing at all times. If they weren't actually watching from outside, they were inside the house."

The young girl who had welcomed Martha so warmly continued to be her self-appointed teacher. "She would come every day and teach me more of her language," said Martha. "She could act out the verbs that had action, like walking or running, acting out the motions to show me what it was. If it was a noun word that she was teaching, she would point it out to me. So in my little black notebook that I always carried, I was filling up the pages very quickly. And Mary Ruth and I were growing our word files together."

Part of the language-learning process involved recording legends told by the people on tape. The team would transcribe these legends and analyze them, figure out what the words were, the meaning of each suffix or prefix and the order in which they occurred.

Martha said, "If there are ten suffixes or prefixes for each word, you've got to consider order--in what order are these used. If you missed the order, the people would not understand the word at all! It was like figuring out a great big puzzle." The young friend helped them understand the words in the legend. Of this process Martha related, "I would let her listen to just a short part, and ask her to tell me very slowly what it said, so that I could write it word by word. She got so good at this that she would not only tell me the words, but also add in the stutters that the original narrator had used, thinking what to say next. But I actually needed the stutters too, because that's actually the way the oral talk is. This was a good way to learn new words and often in the context. If I knew the words around it, I could predict what a new word might mean."

"One day there was a new word, *eenaymatena,* but in the context it could have meant anything. My friend was trying to tell me what it meant, but I just couldn't get it. Finally she said, 'Well, it's as if you are very, very thirsty and there is not any water--and then you are not *eenaymatena.* I finally understood that it was the word for 'satisfied.' That was an abstract word that she could not act out or point to, but she could describe it in the words she knew she had already taught me so that I could get the meaning!

"And that was a very important word to find because you can also use it in a context of not being *eenaymatena,* satisfied in your heart. It turned out to be a very critical word to have as I worked on the New Testament translation!"

The Amueshas were pleasant people to live among, but not everything was 'rosy' in the tribe, as the team found out one morning. Martha told about one of the tribe's bad practices to show how much they needed God's Word.

"One morning we were doing paperwork, analyzing, studying the texts. Usually there were a lot of people in our house, and we would go on studying even when they were there, unless we were helping them with something. But this morning there was nobody in the house, which was queer, but we hadn't thought about it.

"But in the midst of our study, all of a sudden, there was a scream. A child's scream went up through the whole village. It sounded like it was coming from the far end of the compound.

"We had gone to the assignment with the idea of not getting into family troubles or problems, or any kind of a cultural thing that we didn't understand. So we were a little hesitant as to what to do. As the screams kept getting louder and louder, we finally decided that it must be a child that had gotten hurt somewhere, and we should go see if we could help.

"We looked all around outside our door to see if anybody was there, but there was no one, which was strange in itself. Where were all the people? We then decided to walk toward the screams. As we started out the door and hurried down the whole length of the village, we heard the screams coming from an old, deserted-looking house. As we got closer, we could hear a great commotion. It sounded like people were talking very angrily, and there was a lot of noise. But as we got closer to the door and were about to go in, we could hear the shuffle of feet on the ground floor of this old house--bare feet, as the Indians are barefoot all the time--and they were going toward the back of the house. But as we got to the door and looked in, there was nobody except this little child right in the middle of the floor. His screams stopped as we went in, but he was crying and sobbing and was very distraught.

"We sat on the ground beside him to see where he was hurt. We looked him over but didn't see any signs of injury. Unable to figure out what was wrong, we did realize that this little boy had been through something that was very disturbing for him. We didn't know enough of the language to ask him, and he was sobbing so I don't think he could have told us anyway.

"As we thought of a way to make him feel better, Mary Ruth remembered that she had a little shirt that we might give him. Maybe that would help him to get over what had happened. So we got the little shirt and gave it to him, and he just grabbed it as though this was the only thing that he owned, ever.

"It was some time after that when we found out what had happened. The Amuesha people believe that a small child, an orphan child, can bewitch another person and cause them to get sick and die. So they believed that this little orphan boy was doing that by planting fish bones into the ground and covering them up. If the majority of the people believed that he was doing this, making another person sick and the people died, then their remedy was to beat the child with sticks. That is what they were doing when we heard the commotion--a great many adult people were beating this small orphan boy.

"In those days also, another incident happened at the house right beside us, where the head man of the village lived. One night in the middle of the night, we heard this commotion, and we didn't learn until some time later that they were trying to drive away evil spirits.

"So, even though it seemed such a peaceful and beautiful place where we lived in this little thatched-roof house, we realized the great need for God's Word among this group of people.

"By the end of our first five years, we had learned enough of the language to do some preliminary translation in the Gospel of Mark and in Old Testament stories. We had also started literacy classes during this time with a series of reading books, so the people could learn how to read in Amuesha. People were always in our house, because each one was studying a particular literacy book.

"That was the end of our first term. It was time for furlough and I went home. I spoke to some eighty different churches, sharing about our work. Congregations and friends were very interested, and I gained many more prayer supporters than before."

When the day came for Martha to return to Peru, she went to a ticket office in Miami to obtain her plane ticket, as instructed by Wycliffe's Lima office. At the same time a pleasant young man was also there, introducing himself to the clerk with a question, "Do you have a ticket for me? I am Robert Tripp."

"I was assigned to Venezuela," says Bob. "At that point Venezuela hadn't opened up, so I was wondering what to do, when my friend Carlos LeClaire, who was already in Peru, asked me to come down there. They had just started a Spanish course, so I could study Spanish while waiting to go to Venezuela. Wycliffe administration in Lima had approved my plan and arranged for me to pick up the plane ticket from the travel agent in Miami.

"When I told the agent that I am Robert Tripp and I came for my ticket, he looked at me kind of funny and said, 'Well, we have tickets here, but one is for Robert Duff and one is for Martha Tripp.' At that point Martha joined the conversation, and soon we figured out that the names had gotten mixed up somehow. I don't know if that was on purpose or accidental!"

Bob said, "When we realized that we were both going to Peru and we were both with Wycliffe, we sat together and shared a little bit." Martha added, "It was a twelve-hour trip to Lima from Miami in those days with slower planes. We sat together and had plenty of time to talk and get acquainted. I remember telling Bob how wonderful all the tribe work was, just getting carried away with it and having nothing more on my mind than getting back to the work there."

While Martha had been experiencing translation work and living in the jungle learning the languages of indigenous people, Bob's life had been very different. Through the past several years, God had been using the words and actions of various Christians to prepare and guide Bob toward the life and work of a Bible translator. He had served his country in the United States Navy, and after discharge attended Michigan State College in East Lansing, Michigan.

There he met some Christians who introduced him to Intervarsity Christian Fellowship (IVCF) and gave him tracts and cards with Bible verses. He also began to read the Gideon New Testament he had received while in the Navy. He was impressed by the lives and personal testimony of people he met at the social gatherings of IVCF.

Then toward the end of his last year in college, he heard an evangelist who asked the Christians to raise their hands. Bob said, "So I put up my hand. I thought I was a Christian, and even as I put up my hand, I realized that really I wasn't a Christian. I was really under conviction at that point because I had read some verses about the judgment of God. So that evening after I went to bed, I prayed to the Lord and asked Him to save me from sin. I gave my life to the Lord at that point. The next day it seemed that I was a different person."

Bob began to attend the IVCF Foreign Missions Fellowship prayer group, Bible studies and weekend conferences. He said, "I heard about Wycliffe Bible Translators, and I got literature that indicated they thought then that there were a thousand different languages that needed Bible translation. So I began to pray for Bible translators and the Bible translation program of Wycliffe, and eventually I began to give donations to Wycliffe. Then I'd get letters back from the Wycliffe missionaries."

After graduation in 1949, Bob got a job with Ford Motor Company, working in engineering and plant layout, first in Detroit and then in Cincinnati. "But before long I was back in the Navy. I had joined the Naval Reserves and went on a second tour on an aircraft carrier stationed in Norfolk, Virginia. There I came in contact with the Navigators group and became active at the Tabernacle Church which was associated with the Christian and Missionary Alliance in Norfolk."

After two years serving in Norfolk and his final discharge, a friend asked Bob to help out at a Christian Servicemen's Center in Portsmouth, Virginia, and later he was asked to direct the Servicemen's Center in Jacksonville, North Carolina, near Camp Lejeune Marine Base.

While there, he met Max Lathrop of the Mexico Branch of Wycliffe who invited him to come and share with the servicemen and help out at a little retreat. Max was living in Columbia, South Carolina, and was involved at Columbia Bible College. Bob decided this would be a good chance to get a little better acquainted with Wycliffe, so he joined Max for a trip back to Columbia. It was there on the following Sunday when a student preached that Bob realized, "I just felt that God was calling me to work with Wycliffe."

Max told him he should get more Bible training and suggested that he attend the Columbia Bible College Graduate School of Missions for one year. Bob decided to leave his job and do just that. "That was in 1956," says Bob. "I studied one year, and the summer of 1957 I went to Summer Institute of Linguistics (SIL) at Norman, Oklahoma, took the course, and somehow managed to pass it and was accepted to Wycliffe membership."

The following summer Bob attended Jungle Camp in Mexico and then took a second summer linguistics course at Grand Forks, North Dakota, and ended up in Lima, Peru, to work in the purchasing office.

Bob remembered, "At that point we did a lot of buying of supplies in Lima and shipped them out by truck to the Center at Yarinacocha, a five-hundred-mile trip across the Andes Mountains. At that time the local town was very small, and they didn't have a lot of supplies for purchase."

"My next assignment was with Bob Cromack who worked with the Cashinahua close to Brazil. I was asked to go to the tribe with him for a few weeks; and because we did not have enough kerosene for cooking, we stayed for only a little while. But I did get acquainted with the tribal work, and the Cashinahua Indians accepted me very readily as I went on a hunting trip and had a good time with them.

"When I got back to the Center, I met Ray Hart who had been working with the Amarakaeri Indians in the south. He needed a partner for his time out in the tribe, but he also needed relief for the tribal work while he was on furlough, which was coming up the following year. So I went out with Ray for about four months. Then we came back to the Center and Ray went on furlough. I went back to the tribe with several partners over time. Since Ray never did return to the field, I sort of inherited the work with the Amarakaeri.

"The work in Venezuela never opened up. Since we were unable to get a contract with Venezuela, I stayed in Peru. I don't know if I was ever really assigned to the Peru Branch. I don't even know that I was ever permanently assigned to the Amarakaeris. But I just sort of kept right on working, and it was expected that I just take over, but I don't know that it was ever official.

"I did translation work, literacy work, medical work, trading with the Indians and all that's involved for working with these primitive Indians. They didn't even weave. The women would make bark cloth skirts. Before I got there, before the friendly contact with outsiders, the men wore no clothing at all and the women just wore these bark cloth skirts. The older men even knew how to make stone axes. They were truly stone-age people.

"The translators had houses at the Jungle Base in Pucallpa where they stayed when they were not out in the tribal areas. The time spent at the camp was busy with updating and printing script, getting translation checked by consultants, refreshing supplies--a lot of things that could not be done in the tribal location."

Sometimes when Bob came into the Jungle Base, Martha was also there. Bob remembered, "We, the single fellows, lived quite close to the dining room. We had a ping-pong table, so Martha and some of the other girls and other young people would come over to play in the evening. This is how Martha and I got acquainted, and later on we got together on a Friday evening for social time. Social time was a very important activity in our lives to balance the jungle living with the tribes."

"As the years went by, I would pick Martha up to attend the socials and even an occasional movie in Pucallpa. *Ben Hur* was one of them. Pucallpa was seven miles away from the camp and for many years it was just at the end of a jungle road, a little frontier town with dirt streets. Very primitive, but they did have theaters there. We even rode our bikes there, and sometimes a group of young people would go together for a meal or social gathering. So that is the way we sort of got acquainted and got going together and got more interested in each other during the seventeen years," he laughed, "before we got married. During that time I had more than thirty partners, and Martha had quite a few also. So that gives a little idea of our lives there."

Martha added, "Although we were good friends, we didn't push each other; and I'm sure Bob realized from the way I talked about going back to my tribe, that I didn't have any intentions of anything else other than that. I knew that my work was my first commitment and that's what I chose to do. Then some seventeen years later, while I was getting near the end of my translation and actually finished it in the tribe where I was, Bob heard my announcement about that over the ham radio while he had gone out to his tribe to distribute the books that he had translated. That was in 1976."

"That was the year that the Communist government had taken over in Peru, so we were told that we had to be out of Peru by the end of December of that year. While Bob had the chance to distribute what he had translated by that time, I didn't know how I was going to get my translation back to my tribe if Wycliffe had to leave Peru. So that was a serious time for all of us.

"When I got back to the Base Camp at Pucallpa, Bob hadn't gotten in from his tribe yet, but he called me on the ham radio and asked, 'What are your future plans now that you've finished your translation?' Then I received a letter from him through a Catholic mission asking the same question. I replied, 'Well, I have to go to the States.'

"It was time for my furlough. It just coincided with the time for Bob's furlough because we had gone to Peru at the same time, so our five-year terms ended at the same time. I didn't think about that then, but I said, 'Well, I have to go to Dallas where we're going to have the New Testament typeset, so I'm planning to leave here pretty soon.'

"The people were hearing all this out in the tribe, as we could hear each other on the radio. I thought it was queer that Bob was calling me and asking me this when everybody could hear. So I wasn't too sure what I thought about this. But then Bob got to the mission from where he could send a letter and that was the actual proposal. The letter was a surprise because we could not mail letters from the tribal location. We had to wait for the planes to come.

"I thought about it. I liked Bob, but I was not sure that I was really finished with the work. While I did not have the same compulsion that I had before, I had finished the translation. I had gotten the big thing done. As I thought it over and prayed about it, I felt that this could be God's will for me. But I didn't have any way to tell him except by radio, and I wouldn't do that because everybody could hear that. So I told no one on the Base except my partner, Mary Ruth, because we lived together in the same house.

"As I waited at the Base for Bob to come in from his tribe after several days of delays, I decided I would invite him over and give him my answer. But I didn't think about going down to meet him at the plane; it just never occurred to me to do that. When Bob arrived and I was not there to meet him, he assumed that my answer was going to be 'no,' and I sat at home wondering why he didn't come to see me to find out what my answer was. So I finally called him and said, 'Do you want to come over for cookies and coffee?' That is when I gave him my answer."

Bob laughed as he said, "Which happened to be 'Yes!'"

"By this time," Martha continued, "I had published provisional copies of each book we had. translated, the Gospels, Epistles, etc., so there were a large number of believers. In fact, there were ten churches by that time. They were already doing their own preaching and teaching, which they had done right from the very beginning, because I told them I hadn't come to preach, I hadn't come to teach, but I had come to do this translation for them. I felt that if they wanted to take this translation and teach it to their own people, that was for them to do. Although I felt my work on the spiritual part was finished, I still wanted to do a dictionary and a grammar book in this language. I already had all the data.

All I had to do was to get it organized, which I figured I could do being married.

"There was already an Amuesha Bible School taught by the people using the provisional translation. Young men were coming from all over the tribe to study a course of selected verses showing the way of salvation and Christian life. I had gotten this together because it's a little hard for them to recognize this by reading a whole gospel, especially starting in Matthew and read all that genealogy first. This course of selected key verses on salvation would help them understand how to believe and be saved and follow the Lord. The people responded well to this, and I had no qualms about leaving the tribe. In fact, I thought that would be the best thing I could do. I still feel very strongly that indigenous work should allow and encourage the people to do their own thing."

Bob had not yet finished the translation he was working on. "I was pretty well along," he said. "I think I had done most of the first draft by that time but had not finished it."

Martha added, "When Bob and I got our understanding, I suggested that if we were going to get married, we should do it fast. I thought a fall wedding in the States would be ideal because I like the fall season. By now it was already October and we got married on October 28th."

"We decided not to tell the people on our Base, because we had only one week to get ready to leave. We knew that if we told them, there would be all kinds of activities, like a shower and parties while we were trying to get packed for furlough, and I had to make arrangements for the New Testament to be published."

Bob gave this version of their departure. "After I asked Martha to marry me and she accepted, she sort of swept me off my feet and said, 'Oh, we've got to get married right away!'" He laughed, "We had only six days after that, and Martha believed we wouldn't have time to get ready to leave if we told anybody. So we told them just as we were leaving; and since we had not really gone together publicly, people didn't know that we were even interested in each other. When they finally found out, everyone was really surprised but happy for us."

What Bob and Martha have not included in their story is the reaction of the members of the Peru Branch who were at Yarinacocha when they made their announcement as they headed for the airport. Jan Townsend, who was present that day, shared what happened. "We had no idea they were interested in each other," she said. Then she related how the group went to the airport at Pucallpa from where Bob and Martha flew to Lima, so they could throw rice at them. Another friend, Ilo Leach, had already called the Lima office and clued the members there to what was happening, so when this newly engaged couple arrived there, they were greeted in a special way.

They flew to South Carolina to visit Bob's parents first in their brand new home and decided to have the wedding there. The lower level had a large room with a fireplace which would be perfect for a family wedding, they decided. Bob's mother suggested that her Presbyterian minister marry them, but Bob had a Navy buddy who had gone to Bob Jones University and been pastor of a Baptist Church. They had kept up with each other, and Bob knew he was in Greenville, South Carolina. When Bob called him to perform the ceremony, he said, "I'll do it, but I am working on a church building (construction) down in Georgia. But this coming Thursday I'll be there at 4:30 at your place, and I'll perform the marriage." Bob said, "So it was that the minister set the time for the marriage. That was fine with us as we needed the time. I had called him right after we got to my folk's house at Tryon. Then, two or three days later, he called and said, 'Come over for some marriage counseling,' which we did. All of that happened within a week after our arrival in the States."

"We needed the time to get the license, get our clothes, and let the family know about all of this--a marriage that they didn't suspect was coming up. It was a surprise to everybody." Martha added, "Bob's mother wasn't too sure that this old Navy buddy of

Bob's would be the right man to perform the marriage ceremony. She didn't know what this Navy buddy might look like. So she told me secretly, 'Martha, why don't you try to persuade Bob. Our Presbyterian minister would be happy to marry you, you know.' I replied that, 'It would be better just to have who Bob thought we ought to have.' So we ended up having Hubert, Bob's Navy buddy, marry us. He looked all right."

Martha had the groundskeeper get fall leaves for the mantle over the fireplace. A florist provided chrysanthemums in fall colors--yellow and rust color, according to Bob. Martha added, "We didn't even have clothes for this wedding that was coming off so soon. Bob's parents said they wanted to buy our wedding clothes. Bob made the first trip, but by now it was the day before the wedding, and I still didn't have a dress and wondered how I might find one in one day. But Bob's mother took me to a nice department store in Greenville, and the first one I looked at in the formal wear section was a light peach color, just what I thought I wanted. I tried on a few others, but Bob's mother agreed that the light peach color was just perfect. That was really something, to get the wedding dress just the day before the wedding. And more than that, it was a little long, so I had to hem it up and get that done that night before the wedding also. But Bob's mother was so sweet to me. She had me stand up on the stairs, and she sat down on the lower step so she could pin it around in the right place."

So the pretty little wedding took place with only a few family members attending. Martha's parents were no longer living, but her sister from the Knoxville, Tennessee, area and her nephew from Spartanburg, South Carolina, were there, as well as Bob's sister and her son, and Bob's parents.

After the wedding they had a few days' honeymoon at Cherokee, North Carolina, and then began the process of getting the Amuesha New Testament typeset in Dallas, Texas, by Wycliffe's International Publications Services.

Martha remembered that, "This was one of the early New Testaments going through the process at Dallas, and they didn't have programs for all the things I wanted like the layout of the pages. My translation was the first one that was to have double columns instead of script all the way across the page lines, and I wanted footnotes and various other things. Plus a new font for the alphabet of Amuesha had to be created because of the diacritic marks in this language."

"It took a year and eight months for the typesetting process, and even before that, the manuscript had to be typed again because the copy we had brought from Peru couldn't be used. I mean, it had to be re-keyboarded!"

Bob explained the reason for this process. "Martha's New Testament was done on what they called 'Speed.' It was a word processor and it couldn't go from a word processor to a computer automatically. They had to make a printout and then copy everything into the computer. They had to do it twice and then a second person keyed it in again to verify it. If there was a difference from the first time keying it in, the computer would keep signaling for a correction." He explained that, "It had to be proofed again a third time, because the second person who keyed it in sometimes made the same mistake as the first person." Martha added, "That created a lot of proofreading for me, which took weeks to get through. The diacritic marks in the Amuesha language were not known to the typists, so they couldn't recognize the errors. I had to find them."

During the time that the publication was in process, they lived in various areas while Martha did proofreading and Bob worked on his Amarakaeri translation. Although the translation of the Amuesha New Testament was finished in 1976, the date for the dedication was set for 1979. Martha wanted enough time for the word to get out to the Amueshas, as well as other interested people. Martha and Bob returned to Peru after the New Testament had been typeset to engage in the task of arranging for the Bible dedication.

Martha remembered that "Bob was such a help to me in getting all the logistics of the dedication together. You have to think about so many things. Twenty-five people from the United States were expected, and at this time I had moved up into a more remote place in the jungle, the highlands. This area was not accessible with JAARS planes, so I had not thought that any guests could come there."

"However, our friends started writing to say they were coming anyway. I don't remember how many Amueshas came, but the celebration lasted for three days and the local people came and went. It must have been several hundred in all. It was a great time of celebration for them.

"By this time the people had started to wear western clothes. We always encouraged their keeping to their own dress, so everybody wore their original long, tunic-like, coarsely-woven, dark brown robes to the dedication with all kinds of ornaments that they thought were pretty. These could be deer toenails, monkey teeth, or seeds on little strings hanging over their shoulders. They knew just oodles of different kinds of seeds that hardened really nice so that they shake and rattle. These beautiful decorations were especially attractive with their coarse-looking robes.

"Even the men, who by this time had pretty much stopped wearing that original dress, brought theirs out. Some of them had the original woven kind that the older people made before the days when they were able to buy unbleached muslin. The women also wore woven bands across their shoulders, not only for decoration, but also as carrying straps for their babies. I always thought the women were so pretty."

The dedication of the Amuesha New Testament was an exciting time for translators and visitors, but especially for the Amueshas themselves. This was the first time they saw their entire New Testament. They had individual books, so they knew a lot of Scripture already, but it had never before been put together. To have it all in one book made them so very happy.

This Amuesha New Testament was the 100th New Testament to be completed by Wycliffe Bible Translators. In 1995, a special celebration of all four hundred translations completed up to that time was held at the JAARS Center. Martha Duff Tripp, wearing a brown Amuesha *cushma* with rattling seed ornaments on the shoulders, was part of that program. She related how Pedro, an Amuesha Indian in the Peruvian jungle, read to his people for the very first time in their own language Jesus' Words, "I am the way, the truth and the life; no one comes to the Father except by me" (John 14:6, NIV).

Martha quoted Pedro as saying, "This is what we have been looking for! You know how our people have been looking for a message from our 'father, the sun' all our lives. You know how we tried to entice pretty little birds up into our jungle clearing thinking these little birds may have a message from our 'father, the sun.' This is what we have been looking for. Jesus is our Father's message to us!"

Martha also said that before the New Testament dedication in 1979, a provisional form of Revelation had not been published. So it was gratifying to hear a man from the tribe read to his people from Revelation the very first night, right after the books had been distributed.

While attention had been given to completing the Amuesha New Testament and presenting it to the people, Bob still had work ahead of him on the Amarakaeri New Testament. "Thinking back," he related, "I hadn't finished the first draft--probably had gotten halfway through. I was doing exegetical work, preparing a preliminary translation. Martha and I went back to the Amarakaeris for several years. I finished the New Testament in 1985, and it was printed the next year and dedicated. Martha's experience in literacy was a great help in that area. She didn't need to learn that language since she could teach literacy without knowing much of the language."

Martha added, "During the time we were trying to get ready for the dedication, we were working with young adults, teenagers and even younger children. They learned so fast that we got a lot of good readers before the New Testament was ready. Many of the young people decided that they wanted to follow God's Word and kept telling us they wanted to believe. Helping them by choosing relevant verses, they were able to read them to their own people right there at the dedication."

The celebration of the arrival of the Amarakaeri New Testament was somewhat different from the dedication of the Amuesha New Testament. Because the tribal area was so remote, there were no visitors from the United States, but two planeloads of Wycliffe co-workers arrived to celebrate with them. Bob estimated that more than one hundred and fifty tribes people came from the villages.

Bob related that the tribal people wore very little clothing when he first arrived, as they had not had contact with civilization before. At the time of the dedication, they were wearing clothes 'from the outside.' Bob said, "They panned for gold in their area to take down river to buy clothes from traders--even running shoes."

Finally settled at the JAARS headquarters in Waxhaw, North Carolina, Martha wrote and published a book about the Amuesha entitled <u>Jungle Jewels & Jaguars</u>. She is now deceased. Bob worked in some of the JAARS offices, first in the computer center and then in administration. He has now retired, and in 2015 he reported that at age eighty eight he enjoys excellent health, rides a bike and plays singles and doubles tennis, among many other activities.

"I Have Planned It, Surely I Will Do It."

$\mathcal{J}$ ungle Camp in southern Mexico was an exciting, if somewhat scary, new experience for seven or eight couples, a half dozen single ladies, and four young men. For the first six weeks we lived in simple, native-style houses made of sticks plastered with mud scattered around on an almost bare hill. They took turns cooking in the group dining hall over big wood stoves, learning how to make use of native foods and get along with a minimum of canned goods and other staples flown in by small Mission Aviation Fellowship (MAF) planes from the nearest city an hour or so away.

The group had classes in treating medical problems common to tropical areas, giving injections, practicing butchering, and learning how to handle numerous matters we might encounter while living in a primitive area. Going on long hikes, we learned how to handle dugout canoes in the beautiful Jatate River, which separates that part of Mexico from Guatemala.

During that time, strawberry-blond Beverly Hagelie was one of my three housemates. When the time came for us all to move to Advance Base, some of us on muleback with mules carrying our duffle bags, Beverly became my *champa* mate.

We built this *champa* ourselves with some assistance from an Indian helper. We cut cane branches with our machetes and carried numerous armloads for the roof. On one corner was a tree, so we drove large poles in the ground for the other three corners.

Strips of bark connected them to crossbeams. Cane pole beds and tables were tied together with strips of bark. Our stove was a cane framework filled with mud. Jungle Camp staff provided a steel plate for a cooking surface, and we inserted a tin can for a chimney.

Our drinking water had to be carried from the river and boiled. Since we had to find our own firewood, sometimes what we used was not the best. So when we had to dash off to a class, we couldn't be sure the fire had kept burning long enough to boil the water. That was just one of our daily frustrations.

But during the dark velvet of a jungle night with the chirping of nearby creatures and the rustling of dried cane leaves above our heads, Beverly and I were protected from insects under our mosquito net. By then we were comfortable on air mattresses on our cane-pole beds, as we talked before drifting off to sleep.

One night Beverly told me a secret; she was going to get married and go to the Philippines! She would be wife and helper for Bible translator, Elmer Wolfenden, who was already there.

The secrecy was important because Beverly, who had studied linguistics the previous summer, was not yet a member of Wycliffe Bible Translators as the rest of us were. Also, there were still misgivings because she had not known Elmer very long and knew her parents would be concerned about her welfare.

Beverly's home was in Grand Forks, the site of the University of North Dakota. The Summer Institute of Linguistics (SIL) was held there each summer, where young people from all over the United States learned how to recognize and imitate all the possible speech sounds they might encounter on a mission field--sounds not used in English. Committing sounds to writing and learning how to analyze unwritten languages was an invaluable tool before going on a field assignment.

Beverly did not know about this program until Elmer Wolfenden spoke at her church in the summer of 1953. "He shared about his work as a teacher of linguistics," Beverly said, "and his assignment as a Bible translator for the unwritten languages of the world."

"That was the first time I learned about Wycliffe Bible Translators and SIL," she recalled. "Elmer was a good recruiter and he told me all kinds of great things about the organization."

Since Bible school days, Beverly had a desire to serve the Lord full time but had no idea where. After praying much about it, she felt the Lord leading her to at least take the linguistic courses, so she applied to attend SIL during the summer of 1954.

She said, "I knew my parents, committed Christians who had lost three sons as children before I was born, had hoped that I would have a career that kept me near them. I understood their desires, and so I kept my plans from them for a time because they knew that mission training would lead me to a foreign country. The fact that it was with another Christian denomination was also a concern for them. Mom and Dad were very devout Lutherans. Their desire was for me to find a place of service and to marry within the same denomination, so it was difficult for them to see me leaning toward a commitment to another organization, no matter how fine that organization might be."

"But you know what? I was the most miserable person in the world. I was very unhappy about not going to school because I felt strongly that this was the Lord's direction. So now what do I do? I had always been a good girl. I had always been obedient to my parents. And now all of a sudden I was faced with a conflict. It seemed to me a conflict between what the Lord wanted me to do and what my parents wanted me to do.

"Finally, of course, the day came when I had to tell them because I had to be at school in a week. I first talked it over with Dad, and he told me I should do what I felt the Lord wanted me to do, but Mom could not agree. As I anticipated, she talked me out of going to SIL, so I cancelled my registration."

But Beverly had no peace in her heart and felt she was being disobedient to the Lord. She says she was very confused and didn't know who to talk to about her mixed loyalties. "I did not feel that I could go to my pastor," she said, "because he wouldn't want to take sides in a family conflict like this."

Finally she made an appointment with Dr. Pittman, who was the Director of SIL at the University of North Dakota that summer, to explain her situation to him and ask for advice. "He was very gracious," she remembered. "I'll never forget the advice he gave me. He told me I should spend all the time I could with my Bible, looking up verses in the concordance and cross-referencing those that had to do with obedience to God and obedience to parents. He said I should trust to follow in the Scriptures wherever these verses led me, praying that the Lord would show me His will through studying His Word."

He advised her to pray for guidance from God's Word and counseled, "Many years from now, when you have questions about whether you made the right decision, when Satan taunts you that you have done the wrong thing, you can always go back to the promises God gave you in His Word."

"So for several evenings I did this," she said, "and finally a verse in Matthew really got my attention: 'Anyone who loves his father or mother more than me is not worthy of me... Anyone who does not take up his cross and follow me is not worthy of me...' (Matthew 10:37, NIV). Well, that first verse just flew off the page at me. And from that moment I knew that my decision had to be based on what the Lord wanted me to do."

The next day she called Dr. Pittman and told him what happened. Although the course had already been in progress for three weeks, she was allowed to attend and be assigned to tutors to help her catch up with the other students. She would not get university credit, but she could take all the courses.

So she did that. A girlfriend from Grand Forks was also at SIL that summer, and she drove her to the University. "I lived in the dorm," she said, "because there was no way I could live at home and go to classes. I got through that first year and never doubted the Lord's direction!"

Since her parents still struggled with her decision to become a foreign missionary, after graduation she accepted a secretarial position in Minneapolis with the Far Eastern Gospel Crusade, later called SENT. Young people from that organization who had been at SIL that summer had urged her to apply for the job, and she moved to a dormitory at the SENT campus when she started to work. Bev enjoyed that assignment until she went to Jungle Camp.

"During that time the office staff had prayer meetings every day," Bev recalled. "Among the many prayer requests, those from the Philippines were prayed for daily. The Lord used that time to seal in me a real desire to be a missionary. While many people in other countries didn't have Scripture in their own language, my heart was burdened for the Philippines.

"Also during that time, Dr. Pittman had written to Elmer and told him that I was at SIL that summer, so Elmer started to write to me again, and our friendship blossomed! In one of his November letters he asked me if I would consider coming to the Philippines. Well, you can imagine what turmoil that caused. This was a young man I did not know very well. We had dated that one summer, but I knew him to be a fine Christian who loved the Lord. But marrying and going half way around the world, I knew would not make my family happy, and yet I wanted to do the Lord's bidding. So again I went to the Scriptures as Dr. Pittman had told me the first time. Every evening I devoured the Word of God and used the same method of cross-referencing again to find the Lord's direction.

"That same week I was reading in Isaiah," she said, "and the verse I stumbled across included 'I have planned it, surely I will do it' (Isaiah 46:11b, NASB). The last part of that verse in the King James version is, 'I have spoken it. I will also bring it to pass; I have purposed it, I will also do it.' And that verse!--I could not get away from it. It seemed like God just directed me: 'Know that you are supposed to be a missionary in the Philippines,' and on the basis of that, after Elmer had written and asked me to marry him, I wrote back and agreed. And based on that commitment I came to Jungle Camp."

Beverly's tests were not over; however, and it seemed that the struggle of going through Jungle Camp was not nearly as great a struggle as putting God above all else for her, as well as her family. On the way back from Jungle Camp, she stopped at the University of Oklahoma at Elmer's suggestion to meet Bobbie McKaughan and her husband, Howard, who had just returned from the Philippines for furlough. She was to pick up a 'token' from the Philippines.

"So, of course I was anxious to see Bobbie and found out that Elmer had sent me an engagement ring! And that was so very special! The problem was, I could not wear it yet because I was not a member of Wycliffe. I had to be a member before this could become known. So I had to wait. But at least I had something tangible to prove that our relationship was really grounded.

"From there I went back to North Dakota. It was then close to the time for the second summer of SIL and I wanted to attend that. So I moved into the dormitory and took the course. That was the summer of 1955.

"Towards the end of that summer, I was accepted as a member of Wycliffe. That was a happy day! Not only was I an official member of Wycliffe Bible Translators, but I also could go home and put that ring on my finger. And that is what I did! And that proved to be an announcement of our engagement as well.

"Howard McKaughan was the SIL Director that year, and he made opportunities for me to talk to churches in the area to seek support, not only in Grand Forks but in the greater area. I remember one church in particular that was up in the northern part of North Dakota. I had never been there before, but they had a weekend mission emphasis and wanted someone to come to talk about Wycliffe. So Howard provided the opportunity for me and helped me to prepare a message. I had never done this before; I was completely green! Well, well, prepared or not, I went up there that weekend, and, lo and behold, that turned out to be my first promised support, and it was $75.00 a month! The pastor and his wife decided they wanted to support me, which was a tremendous encouragement to me.

"Elmer had written that he wanted me to go to Pennsylvania to meet his family. So, after summer school was over I rode with one of the couples who had been at school to a state I had never visited, to meet my prospective in-laws. It was a happy occasion, and I spent the next couple of months with Elmer's family, getting acquainted and enjoying being with them while doing more deputation. The Lord continued to give me support in many small blessings, and everything confirmed that the Lord wanted me to go to the Philippines. So I was very sure of it.

"Soon it was time to make arrangements to travel to the Philippines. We had decided to get married there because Elmer could not afford to come home and then for both of us to travel back immediately. That would have been a very big expense. So that meant I would be going to meet him in the Philippines at the end of November.

"I took the train all the way from Philadelphia to Seattle, and I really did not want to stop at home. But when I got to Seattle I knew this would be the time to call Mother and Dad because they didn't know anything about my plans. Understanding the sacrifice it would be for them to give up their child and realizing how painful it was for them, I thought it would be less stressful all around if I first told them of my decision over the phone. I told them, 'I want to come home for Thanksgiving, if you can accept what I believe the Lord wants me to do.'

"Mom obviously wanted me home and so she agreed, and I took the train back to North Dakota to spend a couple of weeks with my parents over Thanksgiving. Then I went back to Seattle and flew out to Manila on December 2nd."

It was an exciting time for the Philippines Branch of SIL to anticipate a wedding. But since the date of her flight had been changed so that she could visit her parents before leaving the States, and since Elmer was way up in the northern part of the Philippines, there was no way of getting the information to him quickly. So he arrived in Manila early, expecting her arrival during the latter part of November. The rest of the Branch had joined in the excitement, and when Elmer went to the airport to meet Bev, the rest of the SIL personnel in Manila were with him!

Bev said, "That was quite an occasion! Elmer's fiancée was coming! I got a royal welcome! From then on, two busy weeks of planning centered around creating the wedding dress from material I brought from home. The dressmaker also created two bridesmaids dresses, and I didn't even know who the bridesmaids were going to be at the time, because I really didn't know anybody very well. We were married on December 18th in Manila in a little Lutheran Church. We chose that church to help my parents to be a little more comfortable about the wedding."

"I have known all along that I did the right thing. Yet there were times when we had trials and testing, and Satan did come to me to whisper, 'See, you should have done what your mom said.'"

Bev laughs as she remembers their first Christmas together during their honeymoon. "We spent the first couple of weeks of our honeymoon in Bagio, where we had a little apartment on the second floor. For a special Christmas dinner, Elmer bought a live chicken, which turned out to be a rooster. We had no refrigeration and since we lived on the second floor, we couldn't put the rooster in the backyard. The only place for him turned out to be the tiled bathroom until Elmer butchered him. Elmer knew very well how to do that!"

Continuing their honeymoon, they went to visit the Newells up in the highlands of the country. Bev explained that Elmer would have liked to take her even farther north where a translation had been finished, but that was not possible because it was not safe for a woman to travel four days on a risk-prone river in a canoe.

A month after they were married, Elmer was sent on a language survey of primitive languages along the east coastal area. They traveled to Baler where they were housed with the local mayor, and where Bev stayed while Elmer traveled up and down the coast, being away a week at a time or more. Bev remembers that, "This was when I encountered my first real challenge. I didn't know anyone there, I had no telephone, I had no radio contact with SIL people in Manila whom I had gotten to know. Elmer was gone, and it was the rainy season with storms over the ocean. Elmer was late returning from his trip. Every day I walked to the pier to ask if the boat was expected that day, and the daily reply was, 'Not today.' He was overdue for a week by then, and I had visions of him perishing in the ocean and seeing myself as a widow. That is when I began to claim the verses the Lord had led me to when I made the decision about joining Wycliffe!"

Bev learned that Elmer had just experienced the not uncommon issue with coastal steamers that did not run on any regular schedule, by missing a boat that picked up passengers at his location at 4 a.m. instead of 6 a.m. as scheduled. "So he had to wait for the next boat which arrived four days later!" Bev exclaimed.

"We were on the coast for about a month before going back to Manila. Elmer taught a course in Tagalog to missionaries, not only SIL, but staff of other mission organizations as well. Elmer had written a grammar book on Tagalog, and he knew the language quite well by that time.

"Then we went up north to a group of headhunters, the Ilongot, planning to do a translation there. Another mission organization had been working there evangelizing, but the tribe wanted someone to come and translate the Scriptures for them. We worked on that for a while until Elmer was asked to serve as the linguistics consultant for the entire Philippine Branch. "By the time we were released from the SIL consultant assignment to go back up to the tribe, another SIL-trained translator had been assigned to finish the job, and we didn't need to duplicate the work."

During all this time Bev continued to be concerned for her parents. Her dad died when she had been in the Philippines only one year. Her first son, Steve, was only two or three weeks old, so she could not go home for the funeral. Her concern about her mother caused turmoil for Bev. "Should we go home and take care of her? How serious is her condition? I knew I couldn't get a clear picture from her letters, so I called Mother's sister from the Philippines to share our concerns with her. She advised that we should stay and that she would let us know if Mother needed our help. But my aunt never did call us back."

When time came for their first furlough, a five-week boat trip with their two children brought them to San Francisco and on to the Home of Peace in Oakland, a temporary residency inn for missionaries.

"As it turned out, Mother had a heart attack while we were on the boat. Mother's brother called us the night we arrived and informed us that Mom was not expected to live. So we immediately got plane tickets to get to her as quickly as possible. It was wonderful how everyone responded to our needs and got us on the plane without delay," Bev remembers.

"When we got to Grand Forks, my uncle was there to meet us and took us right to the hospital. Mom knew us. She was in an oxygen tent though and couldn't really talk to us. But she knew we were there and we connected lovingly. That was on Friday and I spent as much time as I was allowed to be with her on Saturday and some on Sunday, and Elmer and I prayed for her often around her bed.

"Her demeanor and attitude seemed to show that she was reconciled and she appeared to be happy for me. She smiled a lot, and I stayed with her Sunday night, very concerned about how ill she was. Then she seemed a little better Monday morning so I went home. I hadn't been home very long when I got a call from the hospital stating that she had taken a turn for the worse. So I immediately went back, but by the time I arrived she was gone. I had walked into the room without seeing the nurse ahead of time, not knowing that Mom was no longer living, but she had the most peaceful smile on her face! I'll never forget that. That smile said to me that she was okay."

Back in the Philippines there were other assignments. Then in 1965, Elmer's study for his doctorate took them back to the U.S. and Hawaii for over four years, which kept them from reaching their final destination, Masbate, until 1972. Bev said, "When we got to Masbate, we found three little islands, the biggest one the shape of a seahorse. The location was right in the middle of the Philippine Island chain. The Masbates lived in the provincial capital of sixty-thousand people, an educated people. It was not a tribal group at all. The Catholic Church had been there for three-hundred years. There were schools, colleges, a big cathedral, hospitals, doctors, lawyers, nurses, but they spoke Masbatene; and they did not have a Bible in what was the 12th ranked language of the country!"

"It was a mixture of dialects and languages, sprinkled with some Spanish words as well. We had a terrible time learning it. Some residents were from Tagalog country up north. Others had come from the Subanos area in the south. Hiligaynon were from the west, so there were three or four different languages that had been combined to make this new language, a trade language.

"We finished the translation in 1992 and it was dedicated in 1994. During all of our service in the Philippines for forty years, I have never been sorry, and I have never doubted for a minute that I came to the right decision to serve with Elmer. There were a lot of struggles, but through it all, the Lord has always been there."

Beverly and Elmer retired in 1994 and moved to the JAARS (Jungle Aviation and Radio Service) Center in Waxhaw, North

Carolina. Elmer published a dictionary and continued to work on materials in the Masbatene language, and Beverly continued to serve as the transcriptionist. Distribution and usage of the Bible remained their focus, which kept them in touch with local translation helpers who reported frequently from the Catholic, Protestant, Pentecostal, and Independent churches--twenty in all, according to Elmer. One of the highlights was a 2014 report from a Catholic priest whose survey showed New Testament usage by seventy Bible study groups in that denomination. Another sign of the continuation of the work is that one of the translation helpers is now working on his own on an Old Testament translation.

Beverly went to be with the Lord in May of 2013, in Waxhaw, North Carolina. Elmer lives nearby with one of his two daughters. One of two sons is now serving with Wycliffe Bible Translators in the Philippines.

"Beverly's struggles with obedience are an indication that God allows things for His purpose that are not always pleasant," shared Elmer in reminiscing about their service together. He credited her diligence as a major contribution to their partnership in God's service as she typed and retyped the New Testament hard copy on location, and then took a fourteen-hour boat ride to Manila twice a year to enter it into a computer at the SIL Center.

"This Is My Daughter. She's Twenty One."

*M*ary Jane and Ron Michaels came together to tell their story, but before starting that, Ron bubbled over with admiration to tell the story of Mary Jane's parents, whom he admired greatly.

He related how Neil and Jane Nellis were among the first recruits for Bible translation in Mexico, having met at the Bible Institute of Los Angeles (BIOLA). Just one week after their marriage in June 1942, they began studying linguistics at Norman, Oklahoma. They were among fifty candidates who left for Mexico after that summer course; and by the end of the year, they were living among Indians who spoke a dialect of the Zapotec language in the mountains of Oaxaca, a southern state of Mexico.

In the years that followed, along with learning the language and beginning translation, Neil and Jane raised four children, but first they had to suffer some disappointments and sadness. In the village where they were living, their first baby, Edward, just six-months old, died of amoebic dysentery. "But this unhappy event presented a real opening for the work there," as their daughter Mary Jane related. "A teacher in the village took pity on these people who didn't know Spanish or the Indian language and had each one of her village children come to the cemetery with little bouquets of flowers to put on the grave site. This just meant so much to my mom and dad as this was at the beginning of their ministry there--a real opening, a breakthrough to the people."

"One of those little boys came to know the Lord. His name was Rolando. It is wonderful to see how God used that time to bring Rolando to the Lord, as well as his mother and some of his sisters. God used my mom and dad to bring so many people to the Lord, starting with Edward's death. Edward was called the sower, because that indeed was what caused the breakthrough to these Indians."

Ron added, "Mary Jane's dad played beautifully on their little pump organ. That little organ had been to China earlier with Jane Nellis' sister, Marguerite Goodner. She met a young man over there named Harry Owen, and they used it in their ministry in China until the Communists came into China and threw them out. The Communists beheaded the Stamms, Henry and Betty Stamm, but fortunately, that didn't happen to Marguerite and Harry. When they returned to the States, they sent that little pump organ down to Mom and Dad Nellis. That was in 1942, and now in 2001 it is still used and still in their home in Oaxaca, Mexico."

"They played hymns when they first went to the village and had little Edward. And when he died, they used that pump organ at his funeral. After that they used it to teach Christian songs to those young kids and the teacher who came; and it became quite a ministry to sing, playing that one musical instrument in the community there, so that was another blessing of the Lord. That's the story of the little pump organ that traveled so much."

Neil and Jane, with the help of the Zapotec Indians, completed the translation of the New Testament into their language in 1970. Their four children--Don, Mary Jane, and twins Dorothy and David--are all serving in missions. Neil and Jane made their permanent home in Oaxaca City until they retired.

But this is Mary Jane's story. She recalled, "I was blessed with living in a godly home and being raised to love the Lord and having devotions. We just thoroughly enjoyed our time in Puebla where I was born. I went to school up to fourth grade there, and then I was in different places up to the twelfth grade. For eleventh grade I was in correspondence school, and twelfth grade I was in Corn Bible Academy in Corn, Oklahoma." She laughed as she commented, "And right next door to it is Fort Cobb, so there was some humor about that--Fort Cobb next to Corn."

"Then, after that I went to Dallas Bible College and studied Bible theology, and I guess I was thinking that would be my major." After one year there, Mary Jane transferred to Rio Grande Bible Institute in McAllen [Edinburg], Texas, across the border from Mexico. There the courses are taught in Spanish, especially designed for Spanish speakers.

The summer after her first year at Rio Grande Bible Institute, Mary Jane went to North Dakota with her parents, who were host and hostess at the Summer Institute of Linguistics (SIL) that summer. She was impressed with the really nice people she met who were taking linguistics training.

"At the time," she said, "I wasn't sure whether I wanted to do that myself. But as we went along through the summer, God spoke to my heart; and I thought maybe I should be doing the same thing because I was raised on the mission field, and I kind of knew the culture in Mexico. So I thought, 'Well, I'll go ahead and train for this also.'" Before the summer was over, Mary Jane had decided to go with Wycliffe and had submitted her preliminary application. For the fall term, she returned to Rio Grande Bible Institute for her third year.

"All along, though," Mary Jane said, "I was praying that I would be able to meet some other person, some guy, because at Rio Grande Bible Institute I had some Mexican friends who wanted to be more than just friends." These Mexican students would serenade Mary Jane and try to convince this blue-eyed blond to date them. "And I said, 'Well, no, let's just be friends.' But I didn't have anybody else. When they asked me, I said, 'No, I don't have anybody.' And they would reply, 'Well, if you don't have anybody, why don't you be my *novia*?' My answer always was, 'I just want to be friends.' It was hard to convince them that that was all I wanted to do. So I was praying for a friend.

"After we left SIL that summer, we went to Houston to speak at a church. We showed slides and my mother sang. I gave my testimony, and afterwards there was a get-together for a summer worker who was leaving.

"This fellow, Ron Michael, was there. I didn't really notice him, although my mother asked a friend, 'Who is that fellow who was sitting in the front row? He seemed so attentive and was taking in every word that we had to say.' The friend replied, 'I don't know him well because as soon as the service is over, he leaves. But he is very faithful; he comes every Sunday.'

"My dad then went over and made conversation with him. Eventually Dad came to get me, and then took me by the arm as I said, 'Dad, where are you taking me?' He replied, 'I want you to meet someone.' To introduce me to Ron, Dad said, 'This is my daughter, Mary Jane. She's twenty one.' He was thinking that maybe there was a possibility of my getting to know this fellow.

"As we started talking and Ron found out that I was interested in missions with Wycliffe Bible Translators, he said, 'Well, I just put my preliminary application in too, to Wycliffe.' My immediate thought was that he could come down to my parents' village and work on the road there because he said that his major was civil engineering, so I mentioned that to him. Actually, he was working as a civil engineer for the highway department.

"He never did do that, but we started writing and our relationship began with that. I'll let my husband tell the rest of the story."

Ron continued, "Well, this is my part of the story. I was raised in a family that was not Christian. My father was Catholic. My mother was Methodist, but she always made us kids go to church. We lived in Houston, Texas, when I was fifteen-years old, and two blocks from my house was Oak Lawn Presbyterian Church. Mother made sure all of us kids attended church there. In 1970 when I was 22, I accepted Christ as my Savior at that church and started to get more involved. I sang in the choir and taught Sunday School for the college and careers group. I started going to the Houston Bible Institute at night and got really interested in somehow serving God. Through a series of events, Scripture and everything, I felt a call to missions and heard about Wycliffe Bible Translators. I didn't know a missionary and hadn't heard about missions before; but through my Bible study at the University of Houston, I met a fellow who had been turned down three times to be a pilot with JAARS (Jungle Aviation and Radio Service), and he had this whole stack of material on Wycliffe. So I took it home, read it, and sent in my preliminary application. I had never met someone from Wycliffe, but two weeks later, at my own home church, I met a couple from Wycliffe Bible Translators. The lady sang. That was Jane Nellis, and her husband, Neil Nellis, played the piano. Then they both spoke and gave testimonies."

"Afterwards, I thought, 'My father used to say, oh, these Christians (he was a Catholic). They just talk about people's clothes and they gossip and everything.' I was determined not to do that. As a result, I would hardly ever talk to anyone. I would just listen to the service and then go home. However, that evening there was a gathering in the fellowship hall, a farewell party for a summer intern from a seminary who had befriended me that summer.

"As I was standing there waiting, Mr. Nellis started talking to me about Wycliffe. Then he went away, and I was still waiting to see this friend of mine who was surrounded by a bunch of people. Then Mr. Nellis came back and said, 'Oh, by the way, have you met my daughter?' Well, I hadn't. She was at the other end of the fellowship hall from where I was. Then Mr. Nellis said, 'This is my daughter, Mary Jane. She is twenty one.' And Mary Jane said, 'Daddy, I'm only twenty!'

"As I talked to Mary Jane, I got fascinated by the story of her life on the mission field and how her folks had translated the

New Testament for a tribal group in the mountains there. That was when I was thinking about going as a support worker with Wycliffe, using my engineering background. I had never met a young lady who was interested in serving the Lord like she was. Here she was, 5'2-1/2" tall and a real pretty girl, and she was going to go out in the jungle and live in a hut and translate God's Word for an indigenous tribe that lived somewhere in a remote area. I was so in awe of this young lady who would be willing to do that. Most of the girls I knew--the girls at church--wouldn't even leave town without letting their hairdresser know, and they had no aspirations to serve anyone but themselves.

"As we exchanged addresses, a fellow tapped us on the shoulder, and we realized that the one-hundred-and-fifty people who were in that room earlier had all gone; and we were just standing there alone, talking. It was the deacon who said, 'Could I please close up the church and go home?' So we went out to the parking lot, and I found out that Mary Jane's mom had gone to Bible Institute of Los Angeles with some members of the church, and that was how they were asked to speak in the church. We found out later Mary Jane's mom and her friends were conspiring outside, wondering, 'Whoa, maybe something is going on between Mary Jane and Ron.'"

Ron continued, "After Mary Jane went back to college, I thought and I prayed. I had been praying for some time that I could meet a young Christian lady. I was so impressed and taken with her, I would say that it was love at first sight, at least on my part. And I think Mary Jane was oblivious to me as a suitor at that time. As we were talking about missions, she was recruiting me as a missionary, and she did a good job because I was recruited and did join Wycliffe."

"I started writing her and remember praying about that. I prayed, 'God, I just don't know what to say. I haven't had much experience with girls. I'm just going to be as bold as I can be.' So the first thing I wrote was, 'Dear Mary Jane, if you're not attached to anyone, not seeing anyone, I'd surely like to get to know you better.' I added a little bit about what was going on, and I signed it, 'In Christ, Ronnie.' Just about a week lapsed before I had enough courage to send that letter.

"Mary Jane had a very good friend from the Mexico Branch named Bonnie Walker. As Mary Jane started reading the letter, she could not make any sense from the first part of the letter because she thought the letter was signed, 'In Christ, Bonnie.' Finally she realized that it was from this fellow she met in Houston, Texas. I'm not exactly sure what she thought at that point."

Mary Jane added, "I just thought, 'What are the chances that this guy is going to write me? He had said he wanted to get to know me better; and if I want to get to know you better.' So I thought, 'Oh, it must be that fellow I met at Oak Lawn Church.' So I read it again in that context."

Ron asked her, "What did you write to me?"

Mary Jane replied, "I was thinking, 'Well, he says he wants to get to know me better; and if I want to get to know him, I need to write back,' which I did. I didn't exactly say, 'I want to get to know you better,' but I'm sure since I wrote back that was enough for him."

Ron continued, "Well, one thing that she said when she wrote back was that she wasn't attached to anyone, and she wasn't seeing anyone, so I knew there was a good possibility to get to know her. After corresponding back and forth, one of our letters crossed in the mail. I told her that my life verse was Proverbs 3:5, 6 (KJV), 'Trust in the Lord with all thine heart, and lean not to thine own understanding. In all thy ways acknowledge Him, and He shall direct thy paths.' Mary Jane's life verse came in her letter, quoting the same verse. Realizing that we had the same life verse and independently quoted it to each other, we thought that was real special."

"Then I decided to go and visit her. Mary Jane was going to an international Hispanic Bible college and seminary. She studied all of her Bible courses in Spanish. I didn't know the implications of that. Here were all these kids away from home, and the staff there had to keep these kids from pairing off and getting together without their folks' permission. As a result, there were very strict rules about being able to see a young lady. In order for me to come and visit, Mary Jane had to have a conference with the dean, who carefully questioned, 'Who is this fellow and what are his intentions? Why is he coming?' I had no idea this was happening. I thought, 'I'm just going to go talk to her.' So when I arrived in south Texas, Mary Jane and I had our first date--two hours, chaperoned, sitting on a sofa in the girl's dormitory with all these girls walking by. We were chaperoned by one of the resident assistants there to make sure we didn't do anything untoward. That was the first date!

"After that short visit, I went back to Houston, and I was pretty sure that she was the one. I'm not sure, but she probably was subject to a lot of picking on by her Spanish classmates about this guy that came all the way down in his little red Gremlin. I had a brand-new, red, American Motors Gremlin that I drove down there. The next time I visited was around Thanksgiving time and Mary Jane's folks came up from Mexico. They had a mobile home on the campus of Rio Grande Bible Institute, and they graciously let me stay there with them. Of course, Mary Jane's mom was eyeing me up and down, questioning me about my belief and what kind of a guy I was. She didn't want just anybody marrying her daughter. I got to know Mom and Dad Nellis, and wow, did I learn a lot about prayer from them! They just had a direct line to the Father, and God would always answer their prayers.

"Mary Jane and I met in August of 1972. In January of 1973 I proposed to her. She wasn't quite sure she was ready for that step yet. She graduated from Rio Grande Bible Institute with a Bible diploma in May of 1973, and then she went back to Mexico with

94

her folks to take a nurses' aide job at a hospital in Oaxaca. She wanted to work at a Spanish hospital because she was going to go into nursing school in McAllen, Texas, the following semester.

"During that time I wanted to go visit her so bad that I was working two jobs, putting in eighty to ninety hours a week to get enough money to go to Mexico. It was the first time I had ever been out of the country. I didn't know any Spanish, and my father, who was not a Christian, was kind of opposed to me marrying a Christian girl. So I moved out of the house when I was twenty five. I got my own apartment and then I set out for Mexico. When I got to Mexico, there was this huge earthquake. I remember sleeping in a house behind the Nellis home. When I woke up in the morning, all of the little curios and artifacts on the shelves were knocked over. I thought maybe some kind of a cat or snake had slithered through, but during the night there was this horrible earthquake near Mexico City. It reached all the way to Oaxaca. My dad was reading the newspaper at home in Houston the next day with my little sisters and brother and mom, not knowing that I was in Mexico. Dad said, 'See, if Ronnie had gone to Mexico, he could have gotten killed in this earthquake.'

"It was the next year that Mary Jane started nursing at the McAllen General Hospital Vocational School of Nursing. During that first term, Mary Jane and I got engaged, and then we got married August 9, 1974, in Alamo Community Church in Alamo, South Texas."

Mary Jane added, "It was a beautiful night for the evening wedding at eight o'clock. I had three bridesmaids and there were three groomsmen. It was a small wedding, but very nice. Before the wedding, my sister-in-law, one of my attendants, kept unpacking my bag, just teasing. When I would go to my room, everything was thrown all over the place, and I had to put it all back again. She must have done this two times. The last time I put stuff back in, I didn't get everything; I think it was some makeup that didn't get in."

"Afterwards, there was a beautiful cake with yellow and blue flowers on top. I had a beautiful bouquet of yellow daisies and baby's breath with carnations and roses. My long white gown and veil were complemented by the bridesmaids' dresses with little hearts imprinted with yellow and blue flowers. The groomsmen wore blue shirts.

"I was baptized at Rio Grande Bible Institute at the age of fourteen when my family was on furlough. Ron's family lived in Houston, so that wasn't far away. We decided to get married there because we also enjoyed the fellowship of the Community Church which we could attend. It was like a non-denominational church, and we really enjoyed the pastor. After the wedding, we went to Corpus Christi for our honeymoon."

Ron recalled, "When Mary Jane threw her bouquet, my brother-in-law came in and said, 'Ron, they've tampered with the motor that we purchased from my brother-in-law, and the car will go only twenty miles an hour. They had this car surrounded, so we decided to take Mary Jane's folks' car. As we went out the front door, while everybody was in the back waiting for us, we drove off. In the meantime my best man, David Nellis, Mary Jane's brother, knowing that we had gone, tried to keep everybody in the back. When they found out that we were gone, they threw all the rice at him. Mary Jane's brother, Donnie, was so mad that they didn't get us because he was in charge of fixing the car up."

"A well-meaning member of the church had said, 'Look, I don't want you to have to go all the way to Corpus Christi at night, so I have arranged and paid for you to stay in a room in a nice hotel in Port Isabel, Texas.' When Mary Jane and I got there, we thought it was like a bad joke. It was a fishermen's motel. There were holes in the sheets, a noisy window air conditioner, and the toilet ran all night, but we didn't care too much. It was our first night together, and the donor thought it was such a great place. I guess he enjoyed time with his fishing buddies there.

"When we finally made it to Corpus Christi, Mary Jane and I had only four days for our honeymoon because that's all they would give her off at nursing school without flunking her. This was Corpus Christi, right on the Gulf of Mexico. We were in the Sheraton Hotel right there on the coast; we could see the ocean and walk down to the shore. Mary Jane all of a sudden started having stomach trouble. About three o'clock the next morning she started having stabbing pains in the lower right part of her abdomen which we suspected to be appendicitis. We rushed to the emergency room of the hospital. They woke up the attending physician.

"After he examined Mary Jane, he came in and had me fill out some paperwork. While I was filling out the paperwork, he said, 'How long have you been married?' I hated to say, 'We've only been married two days,' so I said, 'We've been married only a short time.' As we were filling out the paperwork, all of a sudden I heard this loud crash of metal. I turned around. The door to the medical room next door was half way open, and all I could see was Mary Jane's legs and the hem of her dress laying on the floor. I went rushing in, finding her lying there in a pool of blood. Her face was covered with blood; there was a pool of blood under her head. I thought to myself, 'I've been married for two days and my wife is dead!' So I picked her up and carried her to an operating table, just as the doctor came in. And Mary Jane said that she could not believe, as she was coming to, to hear him say, 'Get the stitch kit.'

"What had happened was Mary Jane was allergic to penicillin. They gave her a mild form of penicillin which caused her to faint, fall, and hit the corner of a metal file cabinet. She needed eight stitches in her forehead and seven stitches on her lower lip. For the remaining two days of our honeymoon she had this huge clot on her lip, and every time we took pictures she had to put her finger in front of it.

"After our two, short remaining days, we returned home to Edinburgh, Texas. We drove down the dusty road to the Nellis' mobile home and as we parked--they had been expecting us--the door burst open, and there's Mom and Dad Nellis and David and Dorothy Nellis all standing happily in the doorway. As soon as Mary Jane opened the door and stepped out, with all these scars and stitches and clot on her face, her mother's mouth dropped, and you can see her concern, thinking, 'What have you done to my daughter?!' Dorothy, Mary Jane's sister, just fell down on the floor howling and laughing at her sister's discomfort, of course. Fortunately, we were able to explain things to their satisfaction. That was our wonderful honeymoon.

"Mary Jane and I went to California for Dorothy and Dan's wedding that summer, and then I went to Moody Bible Institute. I needed a year of Bible study for Wycliffe as part of my training. We spent two-and-one-half years at Moody, where our first son, David, was born. After that we moved to Duncanville, Texas, where we took our first two semesters at the Summer Institute of Linguistics. Our second child, Daniel, was born there and died of aortic stenosis after aortic heart surgery at three-days old.

"We completed our second semester after that. Then we went to Jungle Camp in the spring of 1980. The following summer we attended our third semester of the SIL at the University of Oklahoma at Norman.

"Then we were assigned to work as missionaries in Mexico, but at that time the visa department was no longer giving visas to Wycliffe Bible Translators at the Mexican Consulate there, so we didn't know what to do.

"We were praying and finally the assignments committee of the Members' Relations Department at Wycliffe said, 'How about Colombia?' Neither Mary Jane nor I knew anything about Colombia, but we said, 'If that's where we're needed, that's where we'll go.'

"Mary Jane and I were assigned to work with the Chami people. The accent is on the last syllable. That's why it sounds funny to American speakers. They always want to say 'CHAme' instead of 'ChaME.' We finished the Gospel of Mark, the book of Genesis, I Thessalonians, and Colossians. We wrote a lot of literacy books, over twenty-three titles on history, natural science, and medical books like <u>How to Keep from Getting Cholera</u> because there was a cholera epidemic in Colombia. In every community we worked, God gave us at least one family that came to know Christ. Now there are five little churches that have been started. God led quite a motley crew to do the translation--me, from civil engineering in the States, and a former terrorist named Robert, who helps distribute materials and does discipleship. He is a Colombian who became a believer. Robert's grandmother was a Chami lady, so that's why he had such a heart for the Chami people. One of the Chami witch doctors who came to know Christ also helped us in the translation.

"Mary Jane and I finished eighteen years of service in Colombia. We've been married now twenty-seven years, and she hasn't had too many stitches since then, but we keep each other in stitches."

Returning from Colombia, Mary Jane and Ron retired to live and serve at the JAARS Center in Waxhaw, North Carolina. "At this point, we're hoping to go to Ecuador with the Presbyterian Evangelistic Fellowship to continue the translation of the Chami New Testament and disciple the Christians there," Ron said. "We hope to have seminars for them to take back the teaching to their own communities."

It was during the time they lived in Waxhaw that they told me their story. Their children were getting their education and making decisions about their futures. "We have three fine children," said Ron. "David, the oldest, will be graduating with a degree in Christian counseling. He married a Baptist preacher's daughter and lives in Columbia, South Carolina. Luke turned twenty in

2001, and he's very interested in a young lady, and he and this young lady, Jessica, are thinking about becoming missionaries with Christian Missionary Alliance. We have a thirteen-year-old daughter, Julie." Obviously, their situations have all changed by this time.

They continue to support the Chami people in their effort to translate additional books of the Bible.

"You Have A Ticket. I Suggest You Use It."

*T*his radio message, relayed via e-mail from the western United States over Nairobi to the Sudan, culminated a sojourn of two committed Christians who felt the Lord had destined them to remain 'single servants.'

Wanda Pace never thought that she would be a missionary. Her future seemed to be that of a farmer's wife, teaching high school somewhere in Washington or Oregon State. "But in my senior year in college, a Mission Aviation Fellowship (MAF) couple, who were supported by my church, came home from Mexico and convinced me to go back with them to teach the MAF and Wycliffe children at their location. So I accepted a short-term assignment in 1964 for a year, since I was able to teach Spanish. I did not know much about Wycliffe, but teaching for a year in Mitla and a second year in Mexico City, especially teaching the children of those who worked in language translation in Oaxaca, led me to feel that the Lord was asking me to consider joining the work full time," Wanda recalled.

After training at the Summer Institute of Linguistics (SIL) in 1964, Wanda joined Wycliffe and began to work with the Jimaltepec Chinantexc language project for five years before returning to Dallas to work on her MA degree in 1975. In 1977, she accepted an assignment to join Dottie Herzog for a year in a new work that started in the Sudan. "That year stretched from one to two to three years, when Wycliffe asked if I wanted to stay in Sudan or go back to Mexico," remembered Wanda.

"So I prayed a lot about that and felt that the Lord wanted me to stay in Sudan. We were working primarily in literacy programs in cooperation with the education system in southern Sudan. The local government wanted to teach the 'mother tongue' in the first three years of school. As we prepared teaching materials in a couple of languages, I soon realized that the Ndogo people did not have the New Testament in their language. There were only some Bible stories that had been translated by very early missionaries. Peter Rebigo, a local colleague, had taken the first introductory course in translation principles and worked more or less independently to translate some Scriptures, just checking in with a Wycliffe consultant from time to time. When he realized that I worked with Ndogo in literacy, he began to give me his manuscripts to read and to discuss them with me. This is how I got more acquainted with the translation side of the work."

Wanda returned for furlough to the U.S. for a year in 1984. When she returned to the Sudan in 1985, the civil war had begun again and the government of southern Sudan had a lot of other things to think about besides mother-tongue literacy, so the future of that work was uncertain. She decided to assist Peter Rebigo to finish his New Testament translation, helping with exegesis and grammar checks before submitting the work to consultants. She said, "I did much of the keyboarding and a lot of other practical things to keep the project moving. Peter left to study at a Christian college in Nairobi, and I had been asked to teach there about the same time. That enabled me to work with Peter from 1985 until 1991, with the exception of a year when my parents died and I returned to the U.S."

The Ndogo New Testament was finished by Peter after he graduated from Pan Africa Christian College in 1995. Wanda was able to get a visa to Khartoum to continue to work with Peter during the consultant checks. The New Testament was dedicated in Peter's homeland in June of 2002, but for security reasons, Wanda was not able to attend the dedication.

"During these years," Wanda said, "I felt the Lord was confirming that I was to serve Him in missions as a single person and that I should not expect to get married. Since I enjoyed my work very much and was very fulfilled by it, I wasn't looking for marriage, actually."

But in Nairobi in April of 1998, right after an SIL Branch Conference at a translation workshop to translate Sunday School materials into various Sudanese languages, all of that changed in the person of John Davies, the conference organizer for another mission organization.

John was from a Christian family in Vancouver, Canada. He taught elementary education for several years in British Columbia, married and had four daughters. In 1968, the family went to Colombia, South America, to join a church planting team with New Tribes Mission. After a few years teaching the missionaries' children, he began to work with the International Church of the Foursquare Gospel in church planting. The family returned to Canada in 1979 to allow the children to attend high school and college in their own country. John's wife passed away in 1985, and he remained in Canada for another five years while his children continued their college education and while they were getting established.

"Then in 1990 I came to Africa," John said, "working for one year with a children's home in Uganda. In 1992 I began to work with a group called ACROSS, a Christian relief and development organization, in South Sudan. I was very happy working with ACROSS; it was an ideal situation for me. I had a lot of opportunity to travel and work in South Sudan with different church groups, particularly the Presbyterian Church of the Nuri language group. People would sometimes ask me, 'Where is your home?' and I found the best answer was 'My home is wherever I am.' Being on my own, I didn't have to think about wife or children and traveling. I was free to come and go as the need arose."

It was in April of 1998 that John and Wanda met at the Nairobi translation workshop organized by ACROSS. At that time, Wanda was fifty-five years old and John was sixty two.

Wanda had accepted the invitation because one of the speakers who was on her staff had to cancel, and she felt badly about letting down this sister organization with which they had a lot of contact over a number of years. "So I decided that I'd better go and give this talk myself, which would require about an hour and a half every morning for one week," Wanda said. "I stayed up late every night, worked hard, and got a course together for training Sunday School people to translate materials into their own languages. That is how I met John--although I must say, I think most of the week I didn't even know he was not a married man. Although I knew many people from ACROSS, I had not met him before because he was always in Sudan and seldom in Nairobi, I think."

John, enjoying the opportunity for some social life while in Nairobi, asked Wanda if perhaps she would like to go out for dinner. John recalled, "At the end of the first week, I realized that this nice lady I met would leave soon, and there wouldn't be any more contact. It was so nice to have friends, and I thought in that way we could just get to know each other a little bit and share about the work we were involved in. Anyway, we went to a Chinese restaurant not far from where we lived. As we had supper, I discovered that she was from Washington State and I was from Vancouver, Canada, so we were from much the same part of the world and we felt the same about a lot of things related to the Christian life."

"And also we had a lot of the same background," Wanda added. "John had trained to be a schoolteacher; I had trained to be a schoolteacher. We both started teaching missionary kids before we went into other work. We both started out in Latin America so that both of us had a background in Spanish, though John kept up his Spanish a lot better than I." "Well, I was working in Spanish for close to ten years!" John pointed out in Wanda's defense.

"We talked about these amazingly similar interests at length," Wanda continued. "The next day I wondered, 'Now what is the proper thing to do?' Often, if someone had taken me out for a meal, I would write a thank you note, but you don't want to sound too forward when a man takes you out. So I debated and concluded, 'Just because he is an unmarried man, why should I treat him any different from anyone else. If I want to write him a thank you note, I'll write him a thank you note.' That is what I did and dropped it by the missionary guesthouse where he always stayed in Nairobi, which was only a couple of blocks from where I lived.

"A few days later, there was a knock on my door, and here was John 'just dropping by' on his way walking from his office back to the guesthouse. I invited him in for a cup of tea and more conversation. He invited me to have supper, I think the next evening, at the guesthouse. After supper we played a game of Scrabble, and after another dinner and Scrabble a few days later at the guesthouse, we ended up alone in the dining room. I then realized that the Scrabble game must have been just an excuse for more talking, because we never finished the game. We just sat and shared about the things we wanted to share with each other.

"That may have been the last time we met before he returned to his Base in a Kenyan town with an airplane service to southern Sudan. It was right on the border with Sudan, where all the NGO's (non-governmental organizations) that work in Sudan were based. I think that is when I gave him my prayer card, and he gave me a photo. Then he took me home and gave me a bunch of roses! That was the first time in my whole life I received roses from a man!

"Then he left for Sudan, but much to my surprise, he called me from Lokichogio, an interim stop before entering Sudan. In fact that was the last time we were in contact directly for a number of months because I was due to go on furlough, and I knew he would not be back in Nairobi before I would leave for the U.S.

"Although we started corresponding after I got his first letter from Lokichogio, I never thought this relationship would lead to anything serious, although to me it was surprising how we seemed to click."

John remembered, "While we were meeting and playing those Scrabble games at the Mayfield guesthouse, I think I told Wanda a few things about myself that were, what you might call, 'negatives.' Those are the things in one's life that perhaps you don't tell just everyone, but it's good to talk about before it causes upset later, things about my growing up and my previous work and so on."

"I thought," he said, "when I tell her these things maybe she will not want to spend much time with me after that. But then I remembered that she had shared a few rather personal things about her own life and situation, and I realized that this was a bit more than just the casual friendship. It had become something special."

Wanda added, "And I think one thing I appreciated was that John said, 'It's good to be open with each other, not trying to hide things from one's past or hide how one really feels and that kind of thing.' I really appreciated that, because I know that for many people that's not how they begin a friendship. I thought that was a really good idea, and I was willing to go by that. I felt like it was good!"

"One of the things that I shared," John said, "was that I had a heart attack back in 1990. Even just things like that would be important to share, because that could affect the other person's decision as to whether to allow any friendship to develop or not."

As Wanda prepared to go on furlough in 1998, John suggested that she visit with his daughters as she traveled through or near Vancouver, Canada, and Dallas, Texas, during her deputation visit schedule. He provided the names and phone contacts for all four of his daughters, and Wanda thought, "Oh man, what would I tell his daughters? Why am I stopping to say hello to them? I don't have any excuse to stop and say hello to his daughters. So I told John that I probably would not be able to do that. But later on, after I was home, I got to thinking and realized that I was going to be driving very close to Vancouver on my way from British Columbia toward the Seattle area. So I decided maybe I could phone them and just ask if they had anything that they'd like to send to their father that I could carry back, and that would be a good excuse. So I tried some phone numbers till I finally got hold of one daughter, told her who I was, and asked if there would be a place where we could perhaps meet. I was encouraged when she thought that was an interesting idea."

"We planned to meet at a restaurant of a hotel that I would pass on my way, and much to my surprise, I was greeted by all three daughters who were living in the Vancouver area and their kids. I felt a bit surprised and overwhelmed that they all came at once like that, but we had a nice talk. They were very easy people to talk to while we had a snack in the middle of the afternoon. I took a photo of all of them, and they brought some gifts for John.

"They had questions like, 'How long have you known my dad in Africa?' and I was embarrassed to tell them that it had been only a few months, so I just said, 'Oh, not too long.' I told them that we were engaged in the same kind of work, but I didn't give them any idea that we were anything more than just casual friends."

John continued, "And then it came time for Wanda to return to Africa and we were able to do things together. Our first outing was with another couple to a volcanic mountain an hour and a half drive from Nairobi. Another trip was down into the Rift Valley. As we came into the valley, we could feel the heat of the desert, and at the archeological site we realized we didn't have any water. It had been left behind in the fridge. The oppressive heat in the desert without water was not a good situation, so we turned around immediately and drove back up to Nairobi. But the trip was still a success, because this minor crisis situation helped us to get to know each other and to see how we would react to difficulties."

Around this time in 1999, Wanda was to go to Khartoum to set up a new training program there by the end of the year. She and John realized that would mean the end of being able to see each other because Wanda would be in the Sudanese capital, the government seat; whereas John's work was in the southern part of Sudan which was rebel territory. Travel from one territory to another would be prohibitively dangerous, and so they felt like they would end up being pen pals without much chance of advancing their relationship. "I felt strongly that the work I was doing was the most important thing in my life, so I never considered that I should question that assignment or make any change in it," said Wanda.

"We did have a chance to celebrate John's birthday with one of his friends from Australia who was in the same organization. But I felt really very stressed by the pressure of the work in administration for the language programs and felt I needed to have a break to prevent burn out."

Having opportunity to get away and spend time together in an appropriate manner presented itself as guests of the Rift Valley Academy guest lodges that belonged to the Africa Inland Mission (AIM). Wanda and John were able to have their meals together and still catch up on newsletters and correspondence.

John said, "We would go to the sunrise service so we could look out over the Rift Valley as the sun was coming up, and I think at the end of that weekend, I was very surprised just how comfortable we had felt together--just appreciating the opportunity to get to know each other better." Wanda added, "Actually, I think that was one of the first steps in thinking about a more serious relationship, although at that time I didn't really want to think of it that way yet. John was very appreciative of the meals I planned ahead of time and prepared there, and even though we both worked a lot, we had some nice walks together in the afternoon."

"Some time later, John gave me a book he said he had purchased for his unmarried daughter, and he thought perhaps I should read it. The title was <u>How to Find the Love of Your Life</u>," Wanda added with a laugh.

"Well, I read it thinking, 'I don't know that I'm looking for that, but it might be interesting.' The book ended with questions about what you wanted in a partner. John read the book before I did, and the next time John came back to Nairobi, we compared our notes and found that our ideas were actually fairly similar. While there were some differences, none were very serious."

Later, they planned another weekend at the AIM missionary farm, a Christian retreat that was appropriate for single people, about four hours from Nairobi. This provided more time to be together, to walk, read, write, and discuss their lives--another step and a blessing in their growing to know each other.

Wanda continued, "This was still 1999, and John went on furlough that summer. We stayed in touch by e-mail, cards and letters. Colleagues who knew us in Nairobi did not realize at that time that we had been seeing each other for over a year, because we were always in public places among professional friends and in professional situations. People from the Sudan Branch also did not know that we had developed a personal relationship, unless some might have suspected because we took our meals together." John added, "We had not really tried to hide the relationship, but it seemed like no one really ever noticed, because we weren't advertising it."

Wanda remembered, "Then it dawned on me that I should mention 'IT' to my Director. I didn't think he would like a big surprise sometime later. But since his wife was cutting my hair one day, and we were alone in the house, I shared with her about my relationship with John and asked her to tell her husband, the Director. But I did say that we were not ready to make anything public yet to avoid lots of different rumors in the missionary community. However, they soon went on furlough and never returned to the field. So another director was assigned, and fortunately, he and his wife were good friends of mine. They invited me to dinner and near the end of the evening, I told them about John and our relationship."

"That was an interesting evening because--well, this is a British couple, and the wife was quite outgoing and talkative, while her husband was more like what you often think of as typical British--a man of few words! While the wife immediately exclaimed, 'Oh, this is so wonderful. I've been praying that the Lord would give you some kind of relief from the heavy stress. Oh, I never thought it would be this! Oh, how wonderful!' The husband said nothing! He kept completely quiet and did not utter a single word until later. More than an hour later, as I was getting ready to go, he said something about the 'great shock' he had gotten that evening. I asked, 'What do you mean? What are you talking about?' He said, laughing, 'Well, about what you said. I've known you for twenty years. You've never had a man in your life. This is IT?' I was so surprised that I just had to burst into laughter about his funny reaction. He was actually quite miffed that I should develop an interest in a man without him knowing about it!"

Some months later when John returned from furlough, they had a chance to consider the future as a Wycliffe mission team. John realized that at age sixty three and a half now, he had only limited time to join Wycliffe because at that time the entry age limit was age sixty five. And Wanda wrestled with the thought that God had called her to be single, so why had God changed His mind?

Wanda's intense search for guidance led to a lengthy e-mail exchange with the wife of a former pastor. She felt she could trust her advice and shared her thoughts. Wanda remarked, "Perhaps to some people this would seem strange, but I felt God had called me to be single, so why had God changed His mind? You hear God doesn't change His mind. So could it really be right? Some things I was still not sure about. I was also concerned that as a married person I wouldn't really be able to give myself to the work as much as I had before. I was happy and satisfied with the work and knew that if you are married you have to give first place to your husband. So it seemed almost sacrilegious that you should put your husband before God. These things just bothered me."

As December neared, John, who had always tried to spend Christmas in one of the Sudanese villages, started to plan the time with the people for social interaction, not just business or teaching. But now an opportunity developed to spend Christmas and New Year's in Nairobi in social activities like meals at the Mayfield guesthouse and some ACROSS activities like the Christmas Eve celebration. John and Wanda realized that they could do these things together, even the New Year's conference at Brackenhurst and a four-day event about an hour away from Nairobi. At first they hesitated, particularly about the festivities with the ACROSS people, but then decided to just do things together--go to meals together, and so on, while they had another opportunity to talk and get to know each other better.

Wanda felt that this was a very big step for her, saying, "While I hadn't been hiding anything, I had been fairly careful not to make any show of our relationship. So for us to decide to go to these places where we were with many people who knew us both and to actually hang around together at meals and at meetings, that was big. But I felt if we did not do this, it might be a bit deceitful. By that time we were really thinking more seriously about the future together. But we did not want to announce a formal engagement without talking to his daughters first."

But there was a symbolic expression that Christmas, when John gave her a beautiful gold necklace which she wore every single day thereafter, even after the 'gold' wore off. John felt that this was the beginning of plans that gradually began to include each other.

This was particularly important as it affected John's tenure with AIM and ACROSS, both of which had policies regarding marriage and age sixty five, and neither Wanda nor John were ready to retire. So they contacted Wycliffe Canada, and John applied for membership which would enable both to work with Wycliffe and SIL at least until age seventy.

In the meantime, both had become eligible for furlough in 2000. Wanda felt at that time that since SIL and AIM had its own joint counseling center, perhaps it would be good to talk to somebody there just to see if there was some advice they could give, particularly of how to approach our families. So we did make an appointment with a counselor and shared our background--the way we met, what we had done so far, and our thoughts about the future. We were encouraged when he stated, 'I believe you are going about this the right way, and I don't see any problems in what you are going. I feel that it's now just up to the Lord to make it very clear, but it seems like you've done things in a good, mature, and solid way.' So John left for Vancouver to attend a meeting."

Arriving in Vancouver a week later, Wanda was met by John, his sister and brother-in-law at the airport, and stayed with them since they had enough bedrooms so that they could stay in the same house.

"On the third day after Wanda's arrival," continued John, "I went upstairs, two steps at a time, and then I felt a pressure in my chest. We were scheduled to visit a niece so I suggested that someone else drive the car, and upon arrival tried to rest, but the pressure did not ease. My sister, a nurse, insisted on taking me to the hospital's emergency room where an angioplasty resulted in a stent implant. It took some days to recuperate, and I was so thankful that Wanda was brave enough to continue the relationship with someone who was having these types of problems."

"It was interesting," said Wanda, "because my first meeting with the daughters after we got to Canada was in the hospital, and the other worrisome issue was how this second heart attack at age sixty four would affect his application to join Wycliffe. A visit to the Wycliffe office in Calgary had already been scheduled so we made the trip together. Somebody had lent me an old used car, which took us on a lot of miles that summer. While the Calgary Wycliffe office could not give a definite answer until the candidate committee met, they were very encouraging.

"We returned from Calgary on September 20th, and John returned to Africa while I stayed about a month longer. By this time we definitely wanted to get married, but we had not decided when or where. We had not made any wedding plans, which seemed a bit silly for people who had been on the field as long as we had, who had worked in places like Sudan for so many years, and who knew the situation when it comes to things like correspondence and getting in and out of the country. While Africa seemed to be a logical choice for both of us, the problem was that each of us had hundreds of African friends, and there was no way we could have a small wedding in Africa. The custom there is to have a huge affair with fifteen bridesmaids and flower girls, a feast that lasts all day, open to anyone who might vaguely know you, and who expected to be fed a full meal.

"In fact, I had never wanted a big wedding in Africa or elsewhere. And to complicate things more, John did not stay in Nairobi. He went straight back up to Lokichogio and then back into Sudan. So the only way I could reach him was by radio and that would open our conversations for anyone in southern Sudan to be listening in. So I stewed in Canada about getting married, waiting another year, getting married in Africa or Canada--just what will it be?

"Besides that, I had all my deputation to do, which meant about six weeks of intensive travel. By this time I had gotten my furlough extended till December, which would give me just enough time to rush back to Africa, still without any definite plans.

"At the end of October I heard that John was definitely accepted by Wycliffe. The letter came to me because Wycliffe did not know how to contact John in Sudan. It was then I decided that I needed to make some plans. I tried to contact a few places in Africa by e-mail, which resulted in inadequate or no answers. By then I was too frustrated to pursue the issue alone, so I called John's sister, the one I felt closest to, and poured all of my frustrations out. She felt that a wedding at home would be best so that the family could be there. Although John had mentioned the possibility of a wedding in Africa to his daughters, and they were supportive, in the end it seemed they would have been disappointed if we had done so. So in the end, his sister and I decided that we would have the wedding in Vancouver the first of January, 2001.

"The next hurdle was to send some e-mails to somebody to try to get John a ticket to come back, having just returned to Africa. My sister had given me a large amount of money so I decided we would use some of that to bring John back. I was able to make a reservation for him to be back on December 19th--leaving Nairobi on the 18th--so I sent an e-mail to his office in Nairobi, and said, 'SEND HIM THIS RADIO MESSAGE: YOU HAVE A TICKET TO RETURN TO VANCOUVER ON DECEMBER 18--I SUGGEST YOU USE IT!'"

"Well, I was quick to use it!" said John.

"This was now early December, and John phoned me from Lokichogio to say 'Yeah, it's okay,' said Wanda. I had of course written lots of letters which he eventually got, so he knew about the wedding plans for January, but I still felt kind of bad that I had sort of railroaded through the wedding plans. But it seemed useless to put this off again and again. Now that we had gained his daughters' acceptance, and they had overcome some initial hesitancy, I took that to be a positive sign that God had really cleared the way.

"We decided to have a very small wedding, which seemed to be more appropriate than having a big showy affair. It was not as though I had ever been longing or dreaming of a big wedding anyhow, because I never liked the idea of spending so much money on one day of your life. So we ended up having probably one of the cheapest weddings that's ever been held because I didn't even have a white wedding dress. As it turned out, we had matching African outfits, because I had a nice one made before I went on furlough, and with the leftover cloth, I had asked to have a shirt made for John. John's daughters and their nine children, my sister's daughter and her husband, and some close friends still made a wedding party of thirty five. It was a really nice family time together--very low key, very relaxed and very happy, according to John."

Five weeks after the wedding, John and Wanda headed back to Nairobi. The administration there recommended that they accept an assignment together, perhaps in a different location, so that they could be starting something new together. As it turned out, they ended up staying in Nairobi at the office, which was a good opportunity because they could move back to Wanda's one-bedroom apartment. Wanda still had an old car, and John was, of course, by this time quite familiar with both the apartment and the area, as it was right near the guesthouse where he had always stayed before. They were able to go to the same church as before, see many of the same old friends, and even continue with the work in Sudan. John still had contact with many Sudanese people he worked with before, so the changes in the professional area of their lives were not as vast as it sometimes is for newly married people.

"I guess we can both say that we've been surprised how easy it has been to adjust," said Wanda. "Many people warned me, more than John I think, that it would be difficult to be married at this age, yet I really did not find it difficult. It has been a very smooth transition, and we have a lot to thank the Lord for."

John added, "Yes, we certainly do have a lot to be thankful for. I was surprised how smoothly our lives have blended together, and we are grateful that both of us are doing much better being married than being single, even though we were quite content that way."

Both agreed that coming from similar backgrounds, spending a lot of time together, and talking openly and frankly beforehand about a lot of things, have helped. Being older and not having to establish a career and raise children, they felt have helped them to appreciate each other and enjoy wonderful companionship.

Wanda and John served in the Sudan for another two years with occasional trips to London to teach special courses. John retired in 2009 and Wanda continued teaching at the Canada Institute of Linguistics, a division of Trinity Western University in Langley, BC, Canada. They also had the opportunity for three-consecutive years to teach at Wycliffe's European Training Program in England. Finally in the fall of 2014, Wanda retired from teaching so she could spend more time with her husband of fifteen years. Following a few weeks of travel in the U.S. to visit friends and family, John went to his heavenly home on May 20, 2015.